# BROKEN PROMISES

# BROKEN

## An Unconventional View of What Went Wrong at

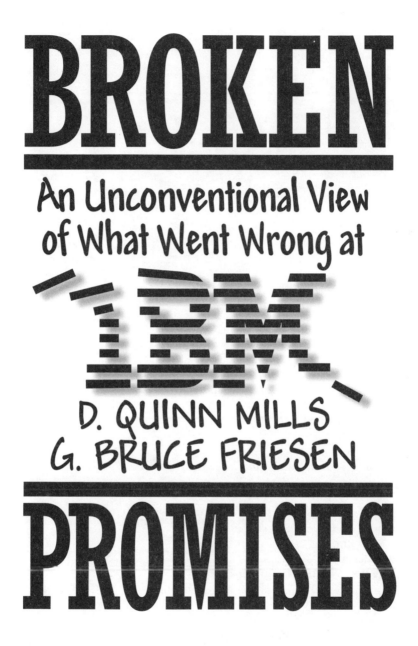

## D. QUINN MILLS
## G. BRUCE FRIESEN

# PROMISES

HARVARD BUSINESS SCHOOL PRESS
Boston, Massachusetts

**Library of Congress Cataloging-in-Publication Data**

Mills, Daniel Quinn.
    Broken promises : an unconventional view of what went wrong at IBM /
D. Quinn Mills, G. Bruce Friesen.
        p.   cm.
    Includes index.
    ISBN 0-87584-654-8
    1. International Business Machines Corporation.   2. Computer
industry—United States.   3. Competition—United States.
    I. Friesen, G. Bruce.
    HD9696.C64I4857 1996
    338.7′61004′0973—dc20                                    95-39965
                                                                CIP

# Contents

# Contents

# Prologue

IBM is making a comeback. Although many observers had counted the company out—a dinosaur, an implosion, a wreck—its revival was probable, even predictable.

Cycles of decline and revitalization have long characterized the company's history. Successful in its established ways, IBM has typically been slow to confront a new technological approach and then has found itself a laggard in need of dramatic change. In times of major technological transition, the company has had to jettison its top leadership and bring in people willing to recognize the need for change and make the break with the past.

Again that has happened at IBM. A new chairman and top management team are now directing the company toward the latest approach to computing—via networks—and IBM is bringing out new products and services designed for networked systems. As Lou Gerstner, IBM's chief executive officer, recently commented, "We are completely transforming the business to address the market for networked computer systems."

But in significant ways, Gerstner has not taken IBM onto a new course so much as to have returned it to its roots. For decades IBM's strategy was to be a one-stop shop for information services for large firms—a strategy we call "singleness." In straying from that strategy during the 1980s, IBM confused and angered its customers. With its current focus on being a full-service provider—G. Richard Thoman,

IBM's chief financial officer, talks of a strategy of breadth, of managing IBM's customers' technological integration for them—IBM has revised the singleness strategy for today's information systems.

To say that IBM's recovery was predictable and that it has followed traditional paths, however, is not to belittle the achievements of its managers. The IBM that Lou Gerstner received was bloated with excess bureaucracy and cost, and its people were demoralized. Initially, Gerstner's management team cut costs and downsized. Profitability returned, but not growth. Over time, however, growth has re-emerged. In 1995, IBM's sales reached almost $72 billion, up more than 12 percent from 1994, and there was growth in virtually all segments of the company. Profitability was also up, by 42 percent, and shareholders were richly rewarded: earnings per share rose by 44 percent. Even new mainframe computers were bringing in substantial profit margins. Clearly IBM has been turned around.

But the company is not completely out of the woods. Sales of mainframes depend upon the business cycle in the economically developed world, and economic growth is slowing. IBM continues to face slow going in sales of personal computers and minicomputers. Its new service units have smaller profit margins than those of the hardware businesses that provided profitability in the past. And the company has yet to restore the confidence of its customers and employees that was so badly damaged in the early 1990s.

The causes of IBM's difficulties constitute a warning to business executives and a source of insight to those who study management and business.

This book, based on extensive interviews with IBM executives and personnel and access to some of the company's files, takes its historical perspective from months of on-site research at the company's headquarters in Armonk, New York. We wish to give special thanks to John Akers, Walton E. Burdick, Ned C. Lautenbach, George Conrades, Jack Riley, and dozens of other present and former IBMers who generously shared their knowledge of IBM with us. We alone, however, are responsible for any errors or omissions in this book.

We have posed a big question about IBM—what happened to IBM?—because IBM is a very large firm in a major industry. We cannot recount everything of significance about IBM: Our work remains only a partial view of the company, and some important topics may go untreated. But we hope we have covered clearly and fully our stated subject: the development and ongoing resolution of the recent business crisis at IBM.

This book should be viewed as one perspective among many that can be taken on IBM. We have stated and supported our position as best we can. We hope our readers will find it valuable.

# PART ONE

# WINNING AND LOSING

# The Market Clobbers IBM

T HE CRISIS AT IBM began innocently enough. Even as the firm's revenue growth slowed and its competitive advantage eroded, most IBMers contently ambled along in their set routines. The firm, too, was content; clouds gathered on the horizon, but IBM continued to set new revenue records each year. Many of its managers argued that real growth would return with renewed economic expansion, pointing out that even though *revenue growth* had fallen off as recession took its toll on prices and unit sales, *total revenue* was still rising; this, they argued, indicated that nothing much was wrong with the company.

Hints of real difficulty first appeared in IBM's dealings with its most sophisticated customers—those firms demanding leading-edge information technology. IBM's newest computers seemed to fall short of meeting the needs of these firms, but rather than examine why this was happening, IBM management appeared instead surprisingly ready to abandon these customers.

After one particularly galling instance of the failure of a new leading-edge product, IBM's chief executive spoke publicly about the gap between the company's stated objectives and its achievements.

> Our greatest mistake . . . is that we walked up to the plate and pointed at the left-field stands. When we swung, it was not a homer but a hard line drive to the outfield. We're going to be a good deal more careful about what we promise in the future.

In the rapid-fire, high-risk world of information technology, the leading edge is a treacherous market, with high costs and razor-thin profit margins. But, it is also the crucible in which ideas are refined and the products forged that will earn huge profits when offered to less demanding customers. That IBM would leave this arena smacked of real trouble to follow.

The press began to describe an IBM in crisis, calling its products dated, its people demoralized, and its managers either hamstrung by rules or running for the exits as their world crashed around them. One reporter noted that "the stock market has been clobbering IBM. The stock has made new lows on heavy volume lately and now sells lower than it did a decade ago." Another wrote that "computer makers are rejoicing at the thought that mighty IBM may have stuck itself well and truly out on a limb."

Within a year, more ominous warning signals appeared. Now new machines in the mainstream product line were slipping in quality. Customers began reporting very late deliveries of new IBM machines, which, once installed, failed to reach anticipated performance levels. IBM's sterling reputation for service and support was being called into question.

Finally realizing the real depth of IBM's troubles—that its bread-and-butter mainframes were slowly but steadily being overtaken by faster, cheaper, and more versatile machines from other vendors and that promises were no longer enough to maintain customer loyalty—the firm's chief executive sent the following message to the management team:

> We are a big company now, but I hope we haven't grown so big that individual managers no longer feel responsible for the total success of the company. With our decentralization, it's very easy to become so concerned with our own immediate responsibility, that we may forget we are all working for the IBM company . . .
>
> Within the last few days, I have talked with two important people anxious to do business with us. These people had been to an embarrassingly large number of places in our company—with no action—before coming to see me. One of them had talked to 18 different IBMers in an attempt to get the answer to a quite simple question. In either case, these men could have been directed to the right person at their first inquiry if the man they approached had simply picked up the telephone and found out who had the information they wanted.

The man cooling his heels outside your office may not look important to you, but this is no reason for not giving him a full, attentive and courteous hearing. Anyone calling on the IBM company should be treated as if he were the most important caller in the world. He might well be prepared to offer the IBM company something that could make him the most important caller in the world, as far as we are concerned. As we get bigger and more successful, it's easy to feel that we don't need the advice or services of outsiders anymore. Let me assure you that nothing could be further from the truth.

It is the business of each of us approached by an outsider to make certain the caller is given the courtesy he deserves and referred to the right person. If you are not the right person, please make sure that whomever you refer the caller to is the person who can give him a full and adequate answer. We have not grown so big, and we are not so successful, that we no longer need the help of others. Nor are we so securely on top that we can all lean back in our chairs and lull ourselves into thinking IBM will go on forever, whatever we, as individuals, do or don't do.

Months passed, but the chief executive's impassioned words failed to inspire action. Recognizing the implications of this inaction, the chief executive and his second-in-command began a series of one-on-one dialogues with various division leaders to prod them into action. These meetings, too, had little effect, and it was with a strong sense of urgency that top management decided to create a committee composed of representatives from across the firm to devise a new course of action.

But bringing IBM's disparate functions together to address perceived problems was like touching a match to a puddle of gasoline. Committee meetings soon degenerated into finger-pointing sessions. When the chief executive proposed overhauling the product line to regain technological leadership, it became apparent that despite three or four years of warning signals, many of his subordinates still saw nothing wrong with IBM that an economic rebound wouldn't cure. The problem isn't in the company, they said, and you shouldn't be pressing for extensive changes. Major elements of the company—manufacturing, sales, and engineering—saw inconvenience and threat in his proposals.

The mainframe manufacturing division did not want to believe that market forces were rendering existing technology obsolete; machines based on this technology were still earning IBM the bulk of its profits. Further, the career, prestige, and compensation of every manager in the group was tied to this technology; they had all grown up on it and would have to reeducate themselves or retire if it was changed.

The sales force strongly resisted the idea of replacing well-known, high-margin computers with substantially different machines with lower margins. Sales compensation was driven by quotas based on margins, and the sales force would have to sell considerably more of the new machines to maintain their incomes. This was, of course, in addition to the effort of reeducating themselves and their customers about the new products.

IBM's engineering managers questioned top management's proposal to pull resources from products in which up to twenty years' effort had been invested. An unstated but very real concern to them was that a new hardware design would require technology based on recent scientific advances that many of them had never studied and so could not immediately understand.

An observer summed up IBM's problems:

> There's the company's persistent difficulty in grappling with the new technology and with the expanding demands of the market. There's the absence of any clear, over-all concept of the company's product line; fifteen or twenty different engineering groups scattered throughout the company are generating different computer products, and while the products are in most cases superior, the proliferation is putting overwhelming strains on the company's ability to [support them]. The view at the top is that IBM requires some major changes if it expects to stay ahead.

Does this profile sound like the IBM of today? It most certainly does. But it's not! The chief executive quoted is Thomas J. Watson, Jr.—not John Akers or Louis Gerstner. Watson's memo on individual commitment to the company, quoted on pages 4–5, was distributed in March 1961; the quotation above came from a September 1966 *Fortune* article, "IBM's $5,000,000,000 Gamble," describing the clash of egos, technology gambles, management disputes, and near-bankruptcy that marked development of IBM's System/360 family of mainframes.[1]

IBM's struggles in the early 1960s sound remarkably like those of the early 1990s. Then, as now, IBM's stock price was falling, smaller firms with more modern technology were eating away at its markets, and the press was hinting at its dire future "if corrective action was not taken"; yet the 1960s were a prelude to the most profitable period in IBM history.

Certainly IBM's recent difficulties have been much more significant than those of the 1960s. The company has reported billions of dollars in losses—its first ever red ink. Its stock market valuation declined at one point by an amount greater than the annual gross product of some of the smaller industrialized nations. IBM has changed fundamentally, making it so unfamiliar to its employees that some have experienced serious psychological trauma. Finally, almost 200,000 people have lost their jobs. No wonder many industry analysts believe that the company is going to crash and burn, leaving only a crater behind.

So today, as in the 1960s, IBM's epitaph is being written; but we believe that today, just as then, it is premature. There is much to learn from what has happened at IBM, both in past decades and recently, and there will be much to learn from its future course.

## WHAT HAPPENED AT IBM?

IBM used to be called the most important company in the most important industry in the world. The stereotypical image of IBM has always been of a monolith, a phalanx in dark blue suits eating the competition's lunch. The editors of *The Economist* have written glowingly of IBM in its heyday.

> IBM was always more the model of an all-conquering American multinational than such other heavyweights as General Motors or Procter & Gamble. It prevailed in every market it was allowed to enter; it was more widely visible, more scrutinised, more admired. It was the lodestar for other companies. Marketing, training, customer and employee relations, research and development—in all these, IBM's way was the best.[2]

The computer industry remains the most important global industry, mainly because ongoing leaps in technology performance and steady cost reductions are transforming our lives. But neither *The Economist* editors nor any other analyst would claim such broad importance for IBM today. Its place in the public eye has been taken by firms such as Microsoft and Intel.

How did this happen? Was IBM a victim of its own success, outgrowing the capacity of even the most capable of managers to run it effectively? Did its basic management techniques become obsolete in today's work environment? Is it the victim of a corporate culture that pushed the wrong type of executive to the top?

## BREAKING TWO PROMISES: A ROOT CAUSE OF DECLINE

In the 1980s, IBM's margins suffered a steep decline, costs remained level, and profits dove. IBM had become a technology follower to an even greater extent than had been typical in the past—a marked change from the 1960s—during which it had led the information-technology industry with its innovative 360 Series. Further, the company displayed a surprising naiveté in its partnering strategies, giving away to Microsoft and Intel extremely profitable portions of the industry and retaining for itself less profitable portions.

These important matters are explored at length in the following chapters, but they are proximate, not root, causes. The decline of profit margins, for example, was due to customers' falling interest in mainframe computers. IBM executives should have foreseen this; that they failed to do so was the result of two other, more basic factors. First, IBM squandered its enormous research and development effort in the 1970s on an effort to build a larger mainframe, instead of developing microcomputer technology, which was about to burst onto the scene bringing with it a future of personal computers, networks, and computer servers. Second, IBM shifted its relationship to its customers and lost touch with their interests and concerns.

What was the root cause of these errors in judgment? How was it that IBM lost the technological leadership it had achieved in the 1960s and became for a brief but crucial period in the 1980s a follower? Finally, after decades of sharp business dealings and building a reputation as the best-managed firm in the industry—many said in any industry—why did IBM executives suddenly made blunder after blunder in dealing with customers and competitors?

IBM's success over many years had been based on two commitments—not formal contracts, but rather understandings based not on legal obligation but on repeated promises. One promise was to IBM's customers; the other to its employees. To its customers, IBM had guaranteed effective, high-quality technology and excellence of service support, maintained by a close and continuing relationship with the customer. IBM rented equipment to its customers and was their partner in data processing and office work. IBM's one-stop shopping ensured large companies that their information systems were up-to-date (though not necessarily state-of-the-art) and reliable. When in doubt, information officers could buy IBM and be confident that their choices could not be faulted.

To its employees, IBM had guaranteed job security. Once a person had a job with IBM, he or she was set for life. Benefits were good; salaries competitive; and the working environment excellent.

Customers were happy, and employees were productive.

But during the late 1980s and early 1990s, IBM abrogated both contracts. IBM's difficulties in the early 1990s—which continue today despite the partial recovery of its share price—have their root cause in the fate of these two promises.

When IBM broke its promise to its customers in order to finance a substantial expansion, its business stagnated. Customers grew angry at IBM's arrogance—its faulty equipment, late deliveries, and failure to keep up with the emerging technology available from other vendors. The company was even castigated for failures in its service—something unthinkable in earlier decades. At the time, IBM's top executives didn't realize that the company was breaking a promise to its customers, and when they did realize it, they didn't care.

When the expansion failed to materialize, IBM broke its promise of security to its employees in order to bail out its shareholders. Breaking this promise impeded IBM's recovery and left its business prospects uncertain. Many employees became disillusioned and ineffective, an avoidable situation. Long allowed by their managers to believe that employment security had little reference to performance, thousands of employees had grown lax, as top performing IBMers complained bitterly in attitude surveys. Had IBM managers dismissed ineffective employees at less than half the rate common at other firms in the industry, it could have significantly reduced its massive financial losses in the 1990s for early retirement and layoffs.

## IBM's MEGASTRATEGY

Behind IBM's two promises stood an overall approach to the marketplace within which narrower business strategies could be formulated,

modified, and abandoned. The two elements of this megastrategy—
what we term *singleness* and *loyalty*—are about customers and people,
because business, even a high-technology business, is about these
things. In high-technology industries, IBM's experience demonstrates
that technology comes third, behind marketing and motivation. In
business, technology is only a means to an end—not the end itself.

### Singleness

Singleness at IBM targets customers, assuring them that IBM can be
their prime or sole source for information technology. So important
has singleness been at IBM, that many observers have remarked, with
considerable justification, that IBM looks more like a marketing than
a technology company. IBM has, in fact, always been a marketing and
service company; despite its commitment to R&D it has rarely been a
technology leader. It has nearly always left this role to its smaller, more
entrepreneurial competitors.

Historically, only when new ideas achieve sufficient prominence to
be of potential interest to the broad marketplace does IBM reassign
engineering and manufacturing resources to developing and producing
its versions of the new product; only then does IBM energize its large
sales force to convince key accounts to accept the new products, with
the promise that IBM's service will remain at the same high level.
Sperry Rand developed the first mainframe; Burroughs devised seamless operating software; Digital pioneered minicomputers; Apple initi-
ated the PC; and so on. IBM copied early versions of these products,
added its own touches, and pushed the results through its top-ranked
sales force—ultimately setting market standards.

This pattern did nothing to endear IBM to its smaller competitors,
who felt that IBM stole the just rewards of their breakthroughs. Otto
Eckstein, an economist, a member of the Council of Economic Advisors
under President Johnson, the founder of Data Resources Inc. (now the
DRI unit of McGraw-Hill), and a director of the Burroughs Corporation,
expressed in the late 1970s the resentment of entrepreneurs toward
IBM. Burroughs was steadily losing market share to IBM, and Eckstein
complained bitterly that "IBM is a public enemy; it's a shark which
destroys innovators."[3]

Ken Olsen, the engineer who founded and led Digital Equipment
Corporation, may have been as bitter as Eckstein about IBM, but he

expressed it somewhat differently. "When technology leads the information technology industry," he said, meaning when new products and services were emerging from development into the marketplace, "then we at Digital do very well. Our sales are strong and our profitability high. IBM does poorly in that environment. But when technology is stable for a while, then marketing, not technology, leads the industry and IBM does very well. We get hurt."[4]

IBM executives confirm Olsen's point from their own perspective, seeing periods of technology change as challenges to their ability to preserve singleness. IBM, they say, for example, never fully responded to the challenge of the minicomputer. Its too long list of incompatible small computers, while containing some excellent machines that sold well, created confusion within IBM and for its customers.

IBM's focus on marketing to key accounts explains why it has such trouble during times of change in the information-technology marketplace. When there is no market standard on which to fasten, ideas from competing factions of entrepreneurs and engineers within the company create bitter internal controversies and paralysis.

## Loyalty

IBM's relationship with its employees, more than anything else, has made singleness possible. Essentially, IBM has fostered employee loyalty to the firm, and IBM's loyal, long-term employees have built lasting service relationships with its customers.

Today's management gurus suggest that firms use value-driven leadership. IBM was using this concept as early as the 1920s. It was formally articulated in a management document in the early 1960s, when Tom Watson, Jr., the firm's chairman, commented that he couldn't manage 300,000 people (IBM's size at that time), but he could certainly lead them. IBM's values were expressed in three fundamental principles of management: respect for the individual, excellence in execution, and the best customer service. Respect for the individual led IBM to embrace a no-layoff practice because it contributed to employee loyalty.

The consequences of this policy have been widely noted. For example, no group of IBM employees in America has ever been unionized, although IBM is a very tempting target. Several years ago, the general president of what was then America's second largest union commented at a conference about the difficulty of trying to unionize IBM. "I once

served on a committee with Tom Watson, Jr., the chairman of IBM,"
he began. "I have never met a more gentlemanly person. He was the
soul of honesty and fairness. If that's the kind of executive IBM produces, then I can understand why we've never been able to unionize
the company."[5]

For decades, IBM has been the place where people in the computer
industry go to work if they place a high priority on employment security. The personal risk-takers go to firms in the Silicon Valley or the
Pacific Northwest. In 1991, when IBM broke its loyalty contract by
laying off personnel for lack of work, it demoralized these employees,
causing some of the best to leave. If downsizing continues, even more
of these people may be driven out, and no company can maintain
standards in the face of a steady loss of its best people.

## A STRATEGIC ERROR OF ENORMOUS MAGNITUDE

Until the early 1990s, recessions in major industrialized countries had
been out of phase: When America went into recession, Japan and
Europe boomed, and vice versa. In consequence, large international
firms like IBM counted on offsetting economic experience in different
countries. In the early 1990s, the first simultaneous recession in each
of the world's seven major economies caught IBM with excess people
and capacity. But IBM had too many people and too much manufacturing capacity for a more fundamental reason. It involved a strategic
planning error made by IBM's top executives in 1981 that cast a long
shadow over the company's future.

The disaster began gently. IBM had been growing at more than
10 percent per year, and the information technology industry was
projected to continue to grow at that rate. In 1980, IBM had approximately $40 billion in sales. In the late 1970s, considerable capacity
had been added and more was coming onstream in the early 1980s.
If the company's growth rate continued, IBM would be a $100 billion
company in 1990. Top executives began to ask themselves if they could
manage a firm that large.

A lengthy period of analysis and discussion followed, at the conclusion of which John Opel, then chief executive, and other company
leaders decided that IBM could and should attempt to reach $100
billion in sales by 1990. To make that possible, the company accelerated

a rapid expansion of personnel and manufacturing capacity that had begun in the 1970s under Opel's predecessor, Frank Cary. More than 100,000 people were added to payrolls; numerous factories and other facilities were built.

John Opel was concerned about the Japanese copying IBM's products and challenging IBM in the marketplace. IBM's salvation, he decided, would be to become the low-cost producer so that IBM could beat Japanese price competition. IBM therefore built automated production capacity, the lowest-cost factories for semiconductors and mainframe computers in the world.

By 1990, IBM was ready to do $100 billion a year in business. Unfortunately, sales were about $50 billion: The company was heavy with unneeded capacity and people. In 1986, at the height of the buildup, IBM had 407,000 people worldwide. By 1994, this number was reduced to only 215,000. Planning mistakes of such magnitude inevitably have major adverse financial consequences—in IBM's case, some $23 billion in special charges were made against earnings, and the company had its first ever red ink. Note, however, that IBM has never taken an operating loss in a full business year. The red ink of the early nineties was all in restructuring charges, the costs of letting people go and closing plants and other facilities.

But was this error, in fact, strategic? Shouldn't it be said that IBM's failure was one of implementation, not of strategy? The industry's rate of growth would have sustained IBM's own target of being a $100 billion company by 1990 had IBM had the products and services its customers wanted. But IBM's top executives had intended to achieve growth through mainframe sales, adding facilities and people for that purpose. When mainframes lost sales volume, the strategy collapsed in ruins. The strategic error was in basing ambitious growth targets on the existing technological paradigm.

## WHEN CRITICS TOOK CHARGE

Having made one egregious strategic error, IBM's top executives followed it with another. Desperately trying to rescue the firm's sinking fortunes and driven by the increasing anger and exasperation of shareholders, IBM went to its critics for advice.

In the past IBM had been so successful that its market value put its executives well beyond the influence of the public equity markets.

IBM's chief financial officer once responded to a question about a possible takeover attempt with the comment "seventy billion dollars [then the value of IBM's stock] is a lot of junk bonds!"[6] What he meant, of course, was that no corporate raider could raise so much money, leaving IBM well insulated from a takeover, the most extreme expression of shareholder discontent. IBM management thus had a fairly free hand to run the firm as it saw fit.

But in the early 1990s, as sales stagnated and restructuring charges turned operating profits into reported losses, the price of IBM stock dropped precipitously. The firm's market value dipped to a point where a takeover was quite feasible, and most of the formerly happy institutional investors became extremely displeased. It was at this point that IBM executives lost much of their freedom of action. Casting about for ways to revitalize the company's share price, they were forced to listen to their critics' suggestions. They discovered that, in today's world, investors' representatives are not content merely to vote with their feet—that is, to sell a firm's shares when they've lost confidence in its management. Instead, they offer management their suggestions, in the form of conditions they set for recommending that investors purchase the stock.

As IBM lost ground, a wave of criticism developed: Its executives were to blame for not abandoning mainframes, for underestimating the market impact of the personal computer, for being arrogant and bureaucratic, and for having a bloated work force. Along with the critique came a solution: Throw out a bunch of people and break the company up! And IBM's executives began to take the advice.

The suggestion seemed plausible enough. IBM had lost to retirement or to other firms most of its senior sales and marketing group, the analysts pointed out; the company couldn't get them or its market dominance back. So, the logic went, IBM executives were mistaken in presuming that they could recreate a dominant integrative-technology company: IBM could no longer provide one-stop shopping for its customers. It ought, instead, to become simply a holding company—a portfolio manager. It ought to divide itself into several businesses and cut them loose to operate independently in the marketplace.

Business magazines printed articles estimating the value of an IBM broken into pieces and divested. Not surprisingly, the separate pieces of IBM were valued much more highly than the company as a single unit. All that should be retained of the old IBM, some asserted, were those parts in which the IBM name had a compelling draw for customers: certainly mainframes and perhaps the IBM personal computer. All else should be separately packaged and sold.

During the divestiture process, the argument continued, IBM's greatest asset would be the huge base of IBM equipment installed and still operating in the world. IBM should turn this base into a service business and milk it for cash, using the cash to invest in new areas of the changing information technology industry. In short, IBM should manage itself like other successful companies, in particular, like General Electric.

Responding affirmatively to its critics, IBM's executives set in motion a process to split IBM into different units. Suddenly there were multiple IBM units. Although the field sales force was not splintered, people in the field no longer understood the company's sales strategy nor felt that they could speak for the company as a whole. While Wall Street applauded, customers became first disillusioned and then angry, complaining of decreased support from their IBM account teams and of increased difficulty in doing business with IBM.

The advice to break up IBM was dead wrong. IBM executives had been handed a conventional solution to the company's ailments, but the critics had overlooked the important point that these suggestions meant junking IBM's decades-old relationships with its customers and employees. Why were these wrong-headed remedies pressed upon the company? The problem lies to a large degree in the analysts' valuation methodologies, which systematically undervalue intangible human and relationship assets while fully recognizing their costs, and in the capital markets' short-term transaction mentality and lack of perspective on the long-term forces. Investment analysts thus project short-term disruptions in technology into long-term disasters and pressure companies to cut costs by driving out the very people who could fix the short-term problems. This policy increases the burdens placed on managers in companies engaged in making wholesale transitions between technologies—as was IBM—rather than supporting them.

This is not what shareholder advocates have in mind when they talk about the discipline of the capital markets. Instead of the arm's-length, buy-or-sale decisions that should influence management by signaling investor disapproval of a firm's performance, leaving the managers to figure out how to do better, IBM confronted a sort of management by remote control. Analysts not only undertook to tell IBM's management to do better, but told them how to do it. Unfortunately for IBM and for its shareholders, management listened.

To his great credit, in one of his first actions as IBM chief executive, Louis Gerstner announced in 1993 that he would not throw a fragmentation grenade at the company—that is, he would not break it up—and, in fact, he has installed a coordinating council of top management to help him pull the company back together.

## WHAT ABOUT TECHNOLOGY?

IBM got into difficulty because it abrogated its contracts with its customers and its employees and because a key strategic error led the firm to overextend. Then it worsened the errors by a radical reorganization that exacerbated the underlying difficulties. These errors resulted in falling profit margins, leaving the company's earnings badly squeezed.

But many observers of IBM tell the story differently. Their version usually insists that IBM fell behind in technology and thereby lost the market.

Did IBM fall behind in technology? The company did cease for a while to be a technology leader, but it didn't fall behind. Yes, IBM tried to hang on to mainframe revenues even as customers were shifting to smaller systems. But mainframes had been highly profitable; why shouldn't the company have tried to stretch out their contribution to earnings? IBM had products in smaller computers, as well, ready to meet changing customer demand. Technology was not decisive.

But didn't IBM lose out on the microcomputer? Not at all—at least, not initially. Apple brought the first micro to market, but it was a poor machine, and IBM quickly responded with its own version. It named the product—the *personal computer*—and quickly grabbed some 90 percent of the market, a share still held by IBM and its compatibles. Yes, IBM did lose most of that share to clone makers, but not because it was late with or lacked the technology.

It is crucial to distinguish at this point between technology and product. IBM had the technology its customers wanted, but because it had lost touch with its customers' needs, it often did not have the product. The weakness of IBM's product line can be exaggerated, however. It had, in fact, strong contenders in each segment of the early-1990s information-technology marketplace. The major products, with the colloquial labels attached to them by IBMers, were mainframes—"beat the Japanese"; RS 600—"the UNIX competitor"; AS 400—"bury Digital"; and networked PCs—"crush Microsoft and Compaq." It was as strong a product line as IBM has ever had.

The myth continues to dog IBM that its current troubles mean that it is washed up as a significant force in information technology—that it can no longer develop leading-edge technology, and that without such technology it will fall behind and fail. In fact, IBM continues to make considerable contributions to information technology. Despite its financial difficulties, the company still maintains an R&D effort nearly equivalent to that of the rest of the industry combined.

## AT THE MERCY OF CYCLES

IBM is at the mercy of three different cycles: an economic cycle of expansion and recession in the major nations of the world; its own organizational cycle of innovation and bureaucracy; and a technological cycle of integration and disintegration in the information-processing industry. IBM benefits when the economic cycle is in its expansion phase, the organizational cycle is in its innovation phase, and the technological cycle is in its integration phase. In the early 1990s, the news was all bad: The world's major economies were in recession; IBM itself was bureaucratic; and the company's existing technology paradigm, built around centralized data processing and the mainframe computer, was disintegrating. It's little wonder that IBM suffered substantially.

In the mid-1990s, each of the cycles is turning. The world's major economies are recovering, and customers are again buying big computers; IBM has awakened itself, and under new leadership is shedding its bureaucratic moss and achieving dramatic administrative and selling cost reductions; and a new technological paradigm—client-server architecture—has emerged and is consolidating itself in a new integrative phase. The confluence of favorable trends in all three cycles makes IBM's future bright.

Singleness prospers as technology consolidates. This element of IBM's megastrategy commits IBM to pulling together for its major customers the divergent elements of information technology. In periods of technology consolidation, IBM's ability to act as a one-stop shop serves it extremely well. What corporate buyer wants to have to deal with many vendors for a single system when one vendor will do?

It had been the instability of technology since the mid-1980s that so damaged IBM. The market standard prevailing since before the 1960s—proprietary, centralized mainframe computing—was cast into doubt, and a replacement did not immediately appear. For all of the hoopla over distributed systems, many major users have adopted a wait-and-see attitude while they try to understand these systems' pitfalls and potential. Until the market standard is clear, a marketing company like IBM is frozen in place; industry leadership slides almost by default into the hands of smaller, technology-dominated firms with a clear point of view—their own technology will win out. The information-technology industry has fragmented into the chaos of open systems, with integrators, software vendors, computer-chip vendors, operating-system vendors, and platform builders all competing for attention, and full-service vendors like IBM suddenly appearing to be dinosaurs.

Unfortunately for the niche players, large-scale users of computing are not technology hounds. Their basic needs have not changed since Thomas J. Watson, Sr., first set out to sell them tabulators back in 1914; they want technology that is functional, reliable, cheap, and easy to use: They want to plug it in, turn it on, and have it work between scheduled service calls. And they want to do business with vendors who can market to them.

Now that the outlines of a post-mainframe market standard are finally appearing through the fog of industry fragmentation, a new opportunity to establish a single solution and to market it on the fundamental basis of cost and service is again in sight. This is a market in which IBM's singleness and marketing focus should again stand it in good stead.

The single solution will best be provided by vendors that can offer truly compatible components—that is, hardware, operating systems, software applications, and service and support designed from the ground up to work together. A fragmented information-technology industry cannot provide such "one-call-gets-all" systems. Software firms like WordPerfect and Borland are already discovering that users want software suites instead of separate spreadsheets or word-processing programs; hardware builders like Compaq or Dell are forced to pre-install software suites—often at cost—to attract buyers. As its smaller rivals seek alliances or mergers in order to integrate their products, IBM is already there: It is the only major player in information technology that remains committed to all five segments of the open-systems marketplace and retains singleness as an operating philosophy.

For all the billions of dollars IBM has spent on new technology, its distinctive competence as an organization has never rested on technology. It is because technology is again yielding to marketing as the driving force in the information-technology industry that IBM, with its focus on providing complete, integrated solutions to its major business customers, can see light at the end of its tunnel. Surveys of IBM's customers done for this book (see Chapter 11) offer evidence pointing strongly to IBM's opportunity. Chief information officers at major companies have a very positive view of IBM. They still see IBM as the firm most likely to deliver the information technology that their companies will use in the future; and, for the most part, they expect IBM to recover its former leadership role in the industry. But the company can still snatch defeat from the jaws of victory.

## A POINT OF DECISION FOR IBM

The market is returning to ground on which IBM is better equipped to fight, but the company must reestablish itself with its customers and employees. Much written about IBM stresses weaknesses in past leadership. But IBM's success depends less on the personalities of its leaders than on correctly assessing the strategic direction in which technology is moving, maintaining—or rebuilding—customer relationships, and motivating its people.

In the customer and motivation dimensions, IBM must make the right choices. In the technological dimension, as big customers move toward distributed systems based on microcomputer networks, with a relatively minor role reserved for mainframe storage hubs, IBM will be in a position to build market share by providing the best price and service—without post-purchase integration headaches.

## WILL BIG COMPANIES REVIVE?

During the 1980s and early 1990s, bigness in business seemed a liability. The adage "the bigger they are, the harder they fall" prevailed. Big firms were advised to break themselves up into smaller units. Executives at large firms envied the agility of smaller firms and tried to imitate it. No large firm seemed to embody the hazards of large size more than IBM.

IBM's experience thus has important implications for the future of all large companies—especially its recent recovery of profitability. Scale, market power, and cash flow still count for a great deal in business; the advantages they give an organization are only blunted—not offset—by the bureaucratic rigidity that so often accompanies them. In today's business climate, the adage is shifting toward "The bigger they are, the harder they *hit*."

Why is it that for several years large companies like IBM were unable to convert the strengths of bigness into marketplace success? First, because overly optimistic strategies were based more on pride than reality. Second, because focus on financials inadvertently crippled other business functions, including often production and marketing. Third, because top executives of large firms came to believe that they could dictate to their customers what to buy, only to discover that they could not. Fourth, because large American businesses broke faith with their employees, and when employee loyalty was lost, they had nothing with which to replace it. Fifth, because when faced with strategic crises demanding tough decisions, top executives fled into reorganizations, leaving the strategic crises unresolved.

Virtually all of these wounds were self-inflicted. A new generation of chief executives, schooled by the errors of the past and committed to correcting them, has assumed the leadership of large firms, and the strengths of bigness are being reasserted. IBM's experience shows that large companies with established customer bases prosper only when they are responsive to the changing desires of their customers. Hence, each decision must be examined in terms of its impact on customers, no matter how unrelated that decision may seem at first glance. Because the conduct of employees is crucial to customer satisfaction—both in product and service—a company cannot cast away the loyalty of its employees without suffering serious repercussions. When loyalty has been lost, performance must be revived by systems that reward employees immediately for success—not in the longer term, as did employment security.

These lessons learned, large companies can survive and prosper. Business history offers few examples of large-scale turnarounds: Ford in 1945, Pepsi when Don Kendall took over, Xerox in responding to Japanese competition, and perhaps Goodyear in 1993. Will IBM be able to do the same, inventing its own course to revitalization, or has it been so damaged by recent setbacks that it will miss the opportunities now looming before it? It is these questions that this book seeks to answer.

# Cycles of Crisis and Recovery

IBM HAS now spent about eight decades—from 1914 to 1995—as a major player in information technology. In its first four decades the tabulator was the market-standard technology; lacking active memory storage, it used cumbersome mechanical relays and punch cards to do a stately four computations per second. The next four decades saw a dizzying series of technology transitions: vacuum tubes and magnetic tape displaced relays and cards; transistors displaced tubes; integrated circuits displaced transistors; and today millions of circuits are "painted" with light onto tiny fingernail-sized chips made out of silicon and other even more advanced materials. The net result has been faster, cheaper, more versatile computing equipment; leading-edge systems now exceed four billion floating point operations per second (FLOPS).

Innovation has created a steady flow of new machines into the information-technology market, each priced well below preceding machines per unit of computing power. Participants in this game play by complex and demanding rules. They must sustain heavy spending on R&D just to remain abreast of technology. They must be prepared to rapidly adjust their organizational infrastructures—often in entirely unexpected directions. And they must sink huge sums into fixed plant and equipment investments with certain knowledge that rapid depreciation will render them worthless in only a few years.

The resulting chaos has been a cannibal's delight; small firms without a rigid infrastructure to hold them back have regularly entered the information-technology industry to eat the market shares of much larger firms that hesitate to change. Over the years, lunch has included the very biggest and best firms—GE, RCA, and Xerox, to name just a few. *Forbes* spoke of GE, for example, in the following terms:

> The term "mess" is not too strong. After almost twelve years of on-again, off-again efforts to win a major stake in the computer business, mighty GE has made discouragingly small progress. . . . Actually, however, the dollar losses are not the biggest part of the problem. . . . What is really ominous to General Electric is the magnitude of the blow to its corporate pride and prestige. Here is one of the most research-oriented companies in the U.S., a company intimately connected with electronics and itself the largest commercial computer user. . . . [Its] chances of ever catching IBM seem to have receded forever.[1]

Until recently, IBM management pointed with pride to a record of orderly increases in annual profits—but the reality of the firm's situation was much more complex. A closer look at IBM's performance suggests that the firm had periodically suffered through bouts of stagnation in the past.

Figure 2.1, covering the period from 1939 to 1990, shows IBM's inflation-adjusted after-tax income and the linear regression of income against time, which portrays IBM as if it were a true public utility with fixed earnings growth set by a regulatory commission. The contrast between the two plots is striking. Although there were several periods—in the 1940s, 1950s, 1980s, and 1990s—when IBM's profits fell well below its long-run average, there has been only one period—1963–1979—when IBM's profits exceeded its long-run average.

Not only does IBM's income fluctuate, but the pattern of fluctuation seems closely tied to technology and economic cycles. The period of prosperity between 1963 and 1979 almost exactly parallels the period during which IBM's 360 and 370 mainframe architectures dominated information technology and the world economy was in almost constant expansion.[2] The periods of underperformance (except for that of the 1940s, which can be attributed to wartime price controls) parallel periods of transition between basic technologies in the industry. Dur-

*Figure 2.1*   IBM's Inflation-Adjusted After-Tax Income

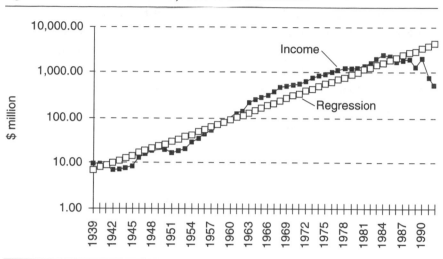

*Source:* Income data from IBM annual reports; deflation data from the U.S. Bureau of Labor Statistics.

*Note:* 1991 and 1992 income data were recalculated to exclude the approximate effect of restructuring charges.

ing these periods, IBM suffered as much—or even more—internal turmoil as did its competitors.

## TABULATORS TO COMPUTERS: ALMOST LOST AT THE START (1948–1954)

From the late 1920s through the 1930s and on into the years of World War II, IBM reaped superior profits from its leading position in tabulator technology. But by the early 1940s, it was clear that this original form of information technology was nearing the end of its useful life. Although demand soared one final time at war's end, many key users, located in urban centers like New York City, faced rising costs to store paper punch cards; they clearly needed a more compact data storage medium than paper. They also needed faster information processing to match their surging volumes of data; some already had entire buildings full of tabulators and punch card storage bins.

New technology—in the form of vacuum tubes and magnetic tape—was waiting in the wings, heralding the demise of the tabulator; but many executives at IBM, including its then chief executive Tom Watson, Sr., refused to believe it. Resistance to change at the top was compounded in the ranks, where people saw the new technology as a threat to their way of life. The firm's profitability was still good, and revenues were rising due to the repeal of wartime price controls—IBM refused to hear the prophets of doom.

IBM had been frantically sponsoring tabulator improvement for years with limited success. Among its best efforts was the wartime Mark I, a giant hybrid machine combining two tons of smaller tabulating units, which ultimately proved too cumbersome for general business use. Meanwhile, the ENIAC, an experimental machine with vacuum tubes for data processing and magnetic tape drives for data storage, was routinely achieving ten times the processing speed of the best tabulator.

But in 1947, when ENIAC's designers sought funding from IBM to commercialize their idea as the Universal Automatic Computer (UNIVAC), Watson, Sr., refused, not trusting UNIVAC's practicality. Vacuum tubes were fragile, and the first computer operators had to keep thousands of them lit in unison; if even one tube in an array burned out, the resulting computations would be full of errors.

It was clear that Watson, Sr., was not going to turn IBM upside down for what he perceived to be a fad. He even turned down ENIAC's patents when they were offered to him. His stated reason was fear of antitrust action; his real reason was a fundamental fear of new technology. He reasoned that if IBM announced a computer development program, his tabulator users would drop their rental agreements and damage IBM's ongoing revenue stream.

IBM's problems were compounded when UNIVAC's designers finally sold their patents to Remington Rand in 1948. Rand was a strong competitor to IBM in tabulator punch cards, with considerable customer credibility and large financial and technical resources. By 1950, Rand had six UNIVACs on order. Meanwhile, IBM continued to dither: after several more hybrid tabulator/computer failures, Watson, Sr., ordered a real computer design, only to balk when he found out that it relied exclusively on magnetic tape. He refused to approve it for fear it would make IBM's punch card business obsolete.

Fortunately for IBM, T. J. Watson, Jr., who became executive vice-president of IBM in 1949, had a clearer vision of the immediate direction of information technology. If the firm was to be about information processing, and not just about building tabulators, he reasoned, then electronics were just a step forward that had to be taken. It fell to him to ease his father out of active management, to point IBM R&D away from mechanical computing and toward electronics, and to grab the chance to mass-produce computers for U.S. air defenses in 1955—all moves that gave IBM a rare second chance to overtake Remington Rand despite its early lead.

In 1948 and 1949, Watson, Jr., revamped IBM's R&D function, adding thousands of engineers with electronics skills to the firm's existing base of mechanical engineers. He also created a separate skunkworks for the new arrivals to ensure that they were not stymied by die-hard managers with mechanical engineering and tabulator development backgrounds. And finally, he approved the release of a small electronic calculator onto the market, IBM's first commercial use of this new technology.

Meanwhile, UNIVAC was pulling steadily ahead. Late in 1951, the U.S. Census Bureau acquired a UNIVAC to test on the 1950 census data; in November 1952, all of America watched a UNIVAC correctly predict the Presidential election on television. IBM had lost nearly four years in the race to bring a commercial mainframe to market.

Once Watson, Jr., had complete control over the company, he placed its full efforts behind the electronic computer. The firm's first real computer—the 701—intended for the Department of Defense, cost $3 million dollars in design alone. It was a huge gamble for a firm whose income had started to stagnate with the loss of market initiative and the onset of the post–Korean War recession; Watson, Jr., nevertheless undertook it.

Nearly two years of hard marketing were needed to place 701s in the first U.S. missile defense system. IBM won this pivotal competition for three reasons: The 701 was intended for mass production, IBM had close connections to the MIT professors who led the crash missile-development program, and it had chits from the government dating to World War II.

The 701 heralded a major shift in computer assembly. Until it appeared on the scene, computers had been treated as hothouse flowers, built on-site from shipped components and large-scale blueprints. IBM reasoned that designing a machine for assembly-line production would drive down costs by pushing the development of standard parts.

As the vendor most capable of rapid production, IBM won the day when the U.S. defense department needed fifty machines in a hurry to guard against a Soviet atomic bomb threat. IBM's superior readiness was widely acknowledged.

> What is needed, obviously, is a machine with an electronic memory . . . in short, a machine that can almost instantaneously reject the safe and highlight the unknown and dangerous. . . . Such a solution appears to be in near prospect. It is a digital computer. Lincoln Laboratory and its partner, International Business Machines, are well advanced on the construction of a prototype.[3]

IBM's second machine—the 702—benefited considerably from the 701. It featured a more reliable magnetic "core" memory, developed at MIT and shared with IBM's engineers, and a more modular design that made it easier to ship and assemble than the UNIVAC. These advantages were touted by an IBM sales force purged of its tabulator veterans. As Watson, Jr., noted about the struggle to overcome UNIVAC:

> If Remington Rand had put their money and hearts behind the UNIVAC right at the start, maybe they'd have been in *Time* magazine instead of us. But nobody at the top of the company had a vision of what computers might mean. . . . Rand wouldn't even let Eckert and Mauchly use his punch-card salesmen to market computers—he said it would cost too much. Instead things were set up so that if a new UNIVAC displaced Remington Rand punch-card equipment, the punch-card salesman lost commissions. At IBM there was never any question—we put the whole weight of our sales force behind our computers as soon as they were announced.[4]

## FROM STAND-ALONE MAINFRAMES TO SYSTEM/360 (1961–1966)

IBM's second crisis, shown in Figure 2.1 by a slowdown in annual income growth to long-run average after 1958, was triggered by computer-industry changes. First, vacuum tubes were yielding to still more compact solid-state transistors; and second, software was becoming more important to computer users who had previously been almost totally concerned with hardware.

Transistors meant more than faster processing; they meant a major change in the existing industry structure. IBM was fundamentally a machine assembler: Because critical electronic parts represented such a small part of a computer's value, IBM bought parts that it did not itself make from vendors like RCA or GE. As these components became more complex, however, the value-added in machine assembly decreased while the value-added in parts fabrication increased. Component makers thus found themselves pushing forward into computer assembly while the computer assemblers found themselves pushed backward into components for competitive protection.[5]

Software compatibility was also an increasing concern. In the struggle with UNIVAC, IBM had made a compromise in its basic computer design. Rather than use an architecture in which the various sizes of computer could run similar software, IBM chose unique designs for each of its models. This allowed IBM's engineers to boost performance with each new machine, but it also forced users to scrap their software each time they changed models. Initially this was a minor concern: Gains in hardware performance swallowed the cost of new software. But the equation changed as users became less willing to junk routines to which they had become accustomed.

As compatibility in software across computer models became the rage, IBM found itself mired in a rapidly aging style of computing. CEO Watson, Jr., decided to leapfrog the market with System/360—an entire line of processors, peripherals, and related equipment that would use a standard operating system (system software). In internal meetings, he confidently articulated his plan to scrap many of IBM's existing mainframe designs and replace them with the single line of different-sized mainframes—but his idea met with a reception that eerily reflected attitudes in 1948.

As Watson, Jr., and T. Vincent Learson, his second-in-command, talked about System/360, no one wanted to listen. Other executives found little cause for worry: IBM still maintained a 75 percent share of market revenue, and no one seemed particularly concerned about compatibility.[6] Watson, Jr., became concerned enough about the situation to issue the memo attacking bureaucracy quoted in Chapter 1. Learson decided that more direct action was necessary. He gathered executives from R&D, manufacturing, marketing, and sales into what became known as the SPREAD committee to push the system idea forward—and touched off a wave of bureaucratic infighting.

In retrospect, System/360 was a huge gamble even for a firm of IBM's size. Fully $5 billion—more than the *cumulative* after-tax profit the firm reported from its creation in 1914 to date—would ultimately be spent in getting System/360 to market. As it would render obsolete all of IBM's existing machines, all existing rentals and service contracts would have to be written off as well. It meant adding plants to the balance sheet and executives and staff to the payroll and unifying the quarreling engineering staff behind one product line.

The pressures of launching System/360 revealed huge gaps in IBM's understanding of computer system development. As IBM had not before focused on software, it did not fully understand how to write large programs. Its response was to break the task into pieces; not surprisingly, these pieces failed to knit when stitched together, and an early budget of $40 million became $500 million in final costs after months of delay and cost overruns. As IBM had never built components in-house, it did not realize the scope of the working capital that would be required. It took all the skills of John Opel—later chief executive—to prevent IBM from going bankrupt as it bought equipment and raw materials on short terms and then found itself unable to rent enough machines to pay the bills. As it was, Watson, Jr., found himself asking for $371 million in equity financing in 1965.

When System/360 was announced in early 1964, some of the "machines" on display were actually plywood models because the real thing was not available. When early versions were shipped, they came in below announced standards due to software flaws.

Not surprisingly, the turmoil called IBM's track record into question. One observer noted:

> The decision by the management of the International Business Machines Corp. to produce a new family of computers, which it calls the System/360, has emerged as the most crucial and portentous—as well as perhaps the riskiest—business judgment of modern times. . . . To launch the 360, IBM has been forced into sweeping organizational changes, with executives rising and falling with the changing tides of the battle. Although the fact has largely escaped notice, the very character of this large and influential company has been significantly altered by the ordeal of the 360, and the way it thinks about itself has changed, too. Bob Evans, the line manager who had the major responsibility for designing this gamble of a corporate lifetime, was only half joking when he said: "we called this project 'You bet your company.' "[7]

System/360 and its successor System/370 ultimately became some of the best-selling computer equipment ever made. IBM's profitability surged forward, and the mistakes were left to the historical record. Or were they? The problems of System/360 certainly influenced IBM management for many years. All of IBM's subsequent CEOs prior to Lou Gerstner—Learson, Cary, Opel, and Akers—had front-row seats as the battle unfolded. It is difficult to believe that it did not shape their views on technology and transition.

## GULLIVER IN LILLIPUT: THE MINICOMPUTER (1978–1981)

In 1978, the era of uninterrupted prosperity at IBM made possible by the System/360 and System/370 mainframe families was drawing to a close. The firm had once again gone into internal turmoil; this time the cause was the minicomputer being pushed by the Digital Equipment Corporation (DEC).[8] Again fundamental change in information technology appeared to be pending, and IBM was slow to respond.

The System/360 and its successors had had considerable impact on the market for information systems: Computing became a game for giants. System/370 machines in particular required users to operate on a huge scale to use them efficiently. Meanwhile, in the shadows, inexorable market forces kept grinding on to produce a machine—the minicomputer—for smaller users.

Minicomputers had actually been conceived in the 1950s. Only after the arrival of cheap integrated circuits in the 1970s, however, could engineers cut the scale of the technology and build hardware priced cheaply enough for small users. Early minicomputers were less capable than their giant cousins, but they were much cheaper to purchase or lease and to operate; as they took shape, the notion that computing was only for giants began to fade away. A new schism developed in the world of information technology. Having previously split along software and hardware lines, information technology split again between big and small systems.

The markets for big and small systems had vastly different dynamics. While there were many times more potential minicomputer users for every potential mainframe user, the mini had a much thinner profit margin. This created a stumbling block in IBM's efforts to sell minis to its customers. What mainframe sales team wanted the headache of demonstrating small machines for small commissions when they could make big money demonstrating big machines?

DEC, lacking so-called big iron, saw the mini as a weapon to break IBM's lock on the computing world. If a small firm used a mini and liked it, DEC could tie more minis onto the first machine and build the user a network. DEC need never fight IBM directly for these first sales, as IBM did not have a strong small-system contender. If the user kept growing with DEC equipment, however, it would never enter the market for the larger IBM systems; it would grow up as a DEC shop.

The proof that DEC had found a winning concept was shown by its revenue curve. By 1975, DEC was exhibiting the same explosive growth that IBM had shown in years past. Once again, the information technology marketplace woke up to the sounds of battle for market position between IBM and a group of upstart rivals.

IBM's chief executive Frank Cary belatedly realized how badly IBM needed a successful small system. Understanding the perverse incentives that led his sales force to favor large systems over smaller ones, he came up with a radical notion—split IBM in half to tackle the two markets. He created new divisions in what had been a single marketing structure: the General Business Group (GBG) for small systems and the Data Processing Marketing Group (DPG) for larger systems.

The theory behind IBM's reorganization was that each division would offer its customers different products. The reality was that the old bugbear of duplicated activity—thought laid to rest with System/360—soon began to plague IBM again. The smaller entities created by Cary promptly attacked each other instead of IBM's external competitors. The carefully separated product lines blurred as price-cutting drove the large-customer data products group onto the turf of the small-customer general business group. When GBG retaliated by bringing out products aimed at DPG's smaller customers, long-term IBM customers became confused about IBM's focus and direction. The following account neatly captured the problem:

As the world's leading computer manufacturer IBM has long had two marketing aims: to maintain its established base of computer users and expand revenues from it; and to expand its customer base at entry level as lowering costs makes it possible to sell computers to ever smaller users. The problem has been that the same cheaper computers needed to bring smaller users within the customer fold can also impact revenues from the existing base by offering them cheaper alternatives for the same tasks.[9]

Selling off the small systems division could not solve the problem. It would only create another DEC-like rival to harass the remaining business. And so Frank Cary attacked the problem in another fashion: He reunified the firm by giving his small systems people a big iron product—the 4300—to sell into their end of the market.

The 4300 was a mainframe offering superior performance to anything else IBM built. To effectively market it through GBG, Cary and his management team decided to give this mainframe a minicomputer price. Not surprisingly, mainframe users queued up in droves to rent or purchase it while waiting for the same stunning price/performance ratio in IBM's larger machines. The impact on IBM's bottom line was equally striking; IBM's inflation-adjusted after-tax revenues dipped for the first time in many years and the firm had to borrow money to finance operations. Its stock promptly sank in value, creating the appearance of instability.

> While giant International Business Machines has been clobbering its competitors with new product announcements, the stock market has been clobbering IBM. The stock has made new lows on heavy volume lately and now sells lower than it did a decade ago when earnings and dividends were one-fourth of what they will be this year. What people once bought on faith they can now buy for yield; it returns 5% on a steadily rising dividend.[10]

This was hardly the image of a staid IBM. The consensus among IBM watchers was that the firm had either gone crazy or was going to crush its competitors—antitrust concerns or not!

> International Business Machines Corp. has long enjoyed a reputation as one of the world's best-run businesses. But that image has taken quite a beating over the sixteen months since IBM announced its 4300 series of medium-scale computers. . . .
>
> Within three weeks of the announcement of the new line in January, 1979, the company was deluged with orders for some 42,000 machines, more than twice as many as it planned to manufacture over the entire life of the series. Delivery schedules were stretched through 1983, well beyond the times when most customers would need the new machines. At the same time, users of IBM's giant computers jumped to the conclusion that IBM's next large-scale systems would offer the same stunning bargains that the 4300 did. So droves of them scrapped plans to buy IBM's existing

big computers and turned instead to leases, which they can cancel when IBM starts shipping the new large-scale systems. . . .

"Our business used to be a lot saner," says an IBM alumnus who now works for another computer-maker. "But IBM hasn't been acting like itself recently and everybody's nervous."[11]

Finally in 1981, another CEO, John Opel, reacted to the crisis by scrapping the separate sales organizations and reconsolidating all of IBM's U.S. marketing activity under one roof. This was not an ideal solution to the problem of internal competition; indeed, it appeared that IBM had proven that large and small computers could not be successfully managed inside the same firm. But as one reporter noted, it was a change for the better:

> [IBM] lost competitive ground through the 1970s—in part, observers say, because it had so many salesmen calling on a single company. . . . [Its] customers were often confused—especially as rapidly evolving technology made product offerings of the three divisions appear similar. It was almost like they were three separate companies.[12]

When the question arose of merging IBM's three different sales organizations (the third for the Office Products Division), it was debated as an issue of merging three different cultures. Could it be done? At what cost? Some staff executives protested, with foresight, that the problem wasn't one of merging cultures, but of the changing relationship between IBM and its customers as IBM switched from rentals to sales. But Opel focused on sales cultures, reuniting the sales force, while insisting "We're in fifteen businesses." Other IBM executives argued that IBM was a single business, though a very big one, and still others maintained that the company was really five or six businesses.

This was an important controversy. If IBM was in fifteen different businesses, it should have decentralized immediately. But Opel failed to act on his conviction, with the result that this significant debate continued in IBM's executive suite without conclusion or consequence.

## WINNING AND LOSING WITH PERSONAL COMPUTERS (1982–1986)

While IBM's financial performance rebounded in 1980 with an easing of the recession and its refusal to keep renting computers—which forced customers to buy machines outright—the respite proved short-lived. The next crisis—desktop computing—was soon upon the firm.

The earliest microcomputer, created in Xerox's research park, was not itself a threat to IBM. The threat was more subtle; desktop computing would reduce the need for time-share, a computing concept that stacked many users on one mainframe with cumbersome hard-wired terminals and central file storage and printing. Time-share had sold many of IBM's biggest mainframes. A smaller and more flexible style of computing would put the giant under pressure once again.

Apple introduced the first commercial microcomputer, and IBM executives studied it with interest and concern. The micro market was exploding, some insisted, and IBM should be in it. At the time, the Office Products Division of IBM, where microcomputers would most naturally find their home, supplied the Selectric typewriter, a single-unit typewriter offered exclusively by IBM for almost two decades. There was no direct competition: Office Products advertised to create demand, and then took orders. By the late 1970s, it had begun to face competition in the marketplace, but still did no product development. The division didn't know how to develop products; nor did it have salespeople who could differentiate for customers their products from the competition's. For this reason the group assigned by chief executive Frank Cary in 1980 to develop the IBM personal computer found a skunkworks in Boca Raton, Florida, outside the firm's mainstream.

To Cary's credit, his efforts got IBM into the microcomputer game before Xerox or Apple could run away with the market. Cary didn't trust the existing product development process any more than Watson, Jr., had many years before. In addition to placing the personal computer program in Florida, Cary exempted the program from normal IBM review procedures, appointed an executive to make essential operating decisions on the spot, and allocated resources so that the team did not have to ask anyone but him for additional money or people.

The end-product of this development program was a huge initial success. IBM's first personal computer models took the market by storm, and within two years of product launch the firm surged from nothing to a market-leading 26 percent share in personal computer revenues. In fact, IBM appeared well on its way to reestablishing its hegemony in the information-technology marketplace.

In retrospect, the trend to small machines had always been there, but it had not been well articulated. With many competing designs floating around, there had been no standard around which a mass market could coalesce. Without a standard, vendors could not gain sufficient volume to create real economies of scale in production, and so unit prices remained high and market demand low.

IBM's personal computer put the power of a huge maker behind a single design. Firms and individuals could now buy a personal computer as an extension of IBM and did so in enough volume to drive costs and prices down. As prices fell, people were willing to buy machines as an experiment, to write software, and to further refine the technology. In so doing, they sparked the personal computer revolution.

### The Open System: What Had IBM Wrought?

Don Estrich's open systems set in motion huge changes at IBM. The team developing the personal computer insisted that they could not use IBM components and still be competitive: It was too expensive, they said. Despite company chairman John Opel's insistence that IBM was the low-cost producer, the Boca Raton group was allowed to go to Intel for computer processors, creating the opportunity for other IBM units to use components from outside IBM. For the first time, IBM put its logo on computer items produced by another firm.

Equally importantly, the Boca Raton group underestimated its sales and their direction. It forecast that 85 percent of its sales would be to home users, 15 percent to business. As a result, it demanded and received retail channels of distribution. For the first time, IBM paid distributors and retailers to sell its products. It charged nothing for the IBM logo, as if it had no value in the marketplace, even though the symbolic value of the IBM logo in the early 1980s was high and should have translated into financial returns.

The team that developed IBM's personal computer has been given accolades by business writers, but it doesn't deserve some of them. A marvelous product development team, their great achievement was producing a machine that took the market by storm and became the industry standard. But they failed as entrepreneurs, failing to capture for IBM the financial potential of their product development. They gave away the IBM logo, undermining IBM's position in the market-place.

These failures with the personal computer were the first visible cracks in the armor of the great company, and more were to follow. Taking the position that it could sometimes get better components outside IBM—and that others could as well—the PC development team published the specifications of their machines and invited other companies to develop products based on these specifications. IBM's twenty-five years of jealously guarding its proprietary linkages were turned upside down. IBM, which once could boast that it had only a handful of competitors—other mainframe producers and Apple—suddenly faced myriads of niche competitors and began to suffer a death of a thousand bites.

It is difficult to understand the motivations at work in the decision to reveal the IBM personal computer design. On one side were the pressures of potential antitrust action, senior management's fear of being left behind as the personal computer took off without a competitive IBM product in sight, and the company's lack of insight into how greatly a successful small machine would transform the information-technology industry. On the other side were the pressures of precedent in the mainframe and minicomputer markets: IBM had never had a nonproprietary product before; the lack of patent protection made cloning too easy and threatened to undermine the firm's position with its key customers. When all the available evidence was weighed, IBM management decided to go with open systems.

There is no evidence that IBM executives thought through or discussed these crucial departures from their traditional business approach in terms of their impact on IBM's huge base of business customers. In fact, some IBM executives explicitly say that customers were not considered. But they were affected—and to IBM's detriment.

IBM has been criticized in the 1990s for having been too slow to accept the open-systems architecture that now prevails in most of computing. But this is hindsight, and it may be a wrong judgment. IBM created an open system in the early 1980s, when the company might have been better served by keeping it closed. It did so first in order to offer a lower-cost product to home users, something that ultimately proved unnecessary since its sales were about 85 percent to business. And second, IBM acted out of the conviction that the market was so big that IBM couldn't expect exclusives. Was this latter judgment correct?

The information-technology marketplace has expanded greatly in the past fifteen years, during which time IBM lost market share dramatically. Some observers argue that IBM lost market share because the market expanded so greatly. Yet clearly, IBM had not expected to lose share. In fact, in 1980 it had planned to grow with the industry in all its aspects, making itself much larger by 1990. Why did this expansion fail? Would IBM have lost even more ground it if had tried to preserve exclusivity? Certainly those who see open systems as an inevitable development think so. But the case is at least debatable that had IBM not abandoned its traditional approach to marketing, it might not have surrendered so much market share to competitors.

IBM was running out of steam in the early 1980s, a time when its financials said it was doing very well. It lost its understanding of the market and its conviction in its traditional approach to its business. It was beginning to embrace third-party vendors instead of close customer relationships and open systems instead of exclusivity. Whatever the merits of these decisions then and now, they ended in financial disaster for the company within a decade.

### The Retail Market: Reining in Frankenstein's Monster

It soon became clear in its handling of the personal computer that IBM did not understand what it had created. The company faced a cruel dilemma in 1982: Should the personal computer be sold more like an industrial product or a retail product? Was it more like a machine tool or a toaster? This was more than an academic debate. If the personal computer was to be treated like an industrial product, the existing sales organization was more or less safe; if it was to be treated like a retail product, IBM needed to reinvent its entire approach to marketing. The early evidence on this point was mixed.

The first IBM personal computers cost thousands of dollars each; they were not typical consumer electronics products. Further, most early users were large firms where the real buyers were the management-information-systems departments placing bulk orders; sales to home users were a tiny fraction of total volume. Key mainframe sales executives argued that the personal computer had a limited potential outside large firms and should be pushed as an add-on product through existing marketing channels. And mainframe sales were again surging as the world recovered from the recession of 1979, giving IBM a familiar headache; two hit products at one time would surely trigger antitrust action.

Eventually IBM disbanded its Boca Raton skunkworks and tied the personal computer to its existing product line. At first the results validated this choice—IBM had its four best years ever from 1981 through 1984. Then the roof caved in. IBM had never seen a high-volume low-margin product before. Strong at selling hardware, IBM had little experience selling software; used to working with engineers in management-information-systems departments, it did not understand users with limited technical skills; finally, IBM did not understand how to get personal computers repaired once they were in the field—it had no experience with retail customers. When personal computer sales exploded after 1984, IBM was unable to keep pace. One user's comments illustrate the problems that piled up around IBM's PC.

Well, the big news is that our IBM PC arrived two days before Halloween. We had paid for it in June, and even after IBM notified us that it had been shipped to the local Computerland there were some, uh, interesting escapades suggesting shuffle and jive, but we do have it. Alas, within days we had major problems. . . .

We bought a bare-bones PC, one disk drive, and 64K bytes of memory. As soon as we got it, we added memory chips, bringing the PC's internal memory up to a full 256K bytes. . . . It turns out there's no trick at all to adding the chips. You have to take the PC apart, but that's a simple matter requiring no tools but a Phillips screwdriver. . . .

However, a day or so after we added the memory chips, the PC stopped working . . . [and back] out to Woodland Hills Computerland went our [machine]. They had it fixed the next day. Seems it was one of our chips. "How can that be?" I asked. "We set the switches to eliminate that memory." . . .

[M]y son Alex wants to call our PC Lucy Van Pelt because it's a definite fussbudget. Two major repairs in a week! Plus a defective master disk, spurious errors, and we had to wait for it four months after we paid.[13]

In 1986, as IBM's PC market share was being undermined by its inability to market these machines effectively in a burgeoning retail environment, its decision to adopt open systems for the personal computer came back to haunt it. In pursuit of open systems, IBM had commissioned a computer chip from Intel and a personal computer operating system from Microsoft founders Bill Gates and Paul Allen. The magnitude of IBM's folly was apparent only with hindsight. When IBM declined Bill Gates's offer to sell it control of MS/DOS, Compaq promptly licensed MS/DOS, purchased chips from Intel, and cloned IBM's machines. The result was a heavy blow to IBM's position in the PC market. One writer described the challenge to IBM this way:

> The Compaq computer is a full-function portable business computer that resembles the IBM PC in almost every way. Not only did Compaq obtain a license to use Microsoft's MS-DOS, but the company's designers also wrote the low-level systems functions used by BASIC into the operating system from the specifications required by the higher-level software. By rewriting instead of copying the code, the designers circumvented copyright infringement yet still created a computer that can run IBM PC software. . . . The Compaq computer has everything going for it—design, compatibility, portability, and price. The only possible obstacle Compaq faces is IBM itself.[14]

Belatedly realizing how important closed architecture had been to its past success, IBM tried to introduce proprietary features on later personal computer models, but market dynamics were now working against it. Open systems were stimulating the market, much to IBM's chagrin, as one writer noted:

> Compatibility with the IBM PC has been a contraposition for IBM. Wide availability of machines that can all run the same software has prompted the creation of thousands of programs. The availability of this software has assured the sale of machines that will run all these great programs. IBM's problem has been that other companies can provide this now-standard computer more cheaply than IBM.[15]

Thus IBM came to the threshold of the 1990s. Its highly profitable mainframes still dominated their market, but that market was beginning to fade. IBM had seized, then lost, control of the personal computer market. It had brilliantly implemented its personal computer strategy; unfortunately, it was the wrong strategy. Some of the firm's most profitable years were still in the immediate future, but so too was the edge of a cliff over which the company was to stumble.

# The Paradox of Success

P ERHAPS THE most important point about IBM's recent flood of red ink
is that although it is clearly an extremely serious situation, it is by no
means the only crisis that the firm has weathered. The transitions from
selling tabulators to selling the 701 computer and from selling stand-
alone mainframes to selling the System/360 family of mainframes
created crises that, when considered in the context of the much smaller
IBM of the 1950s and 1960s, demonstrate that the problems IBM has
faced more recently are nearly proportional to the size and scope of
the organization that must deal with them.

IBM, often its own worst enemy, offers a fascinating example of the
dynamics of innovation and bureaucracy—of healthy growth alternat-
ing with worrisome stagnation—in the life of a single enterprise. Understanding how and why this alternation occurs provides insight into the
workings of modern organizations. Many firms other than IBM have
found themselves in similar straits, and many have not recovered.

## STRUGGLING WITH BUREAUCRACY

Every IBM chief executive has faced the challenge of invigorating the
firm by countering complacency and ineffectiveness among the firm's
staff. In 1949, for example, T. J. Watson, Jr., then executive vice-president, faced entrenched attitudes in his efforts to move IBM from punch
cards to magnetic tape.

I didn't think it would be prudent to run to Dad with the idea that punch cards were dying. He'd have thrown me out of his office. Instead I used a systematic approach that I knew would make sense to the old man. In 1949 I organized a task force of eighteen of our best systems experts to study whether we should add magnetic tape to our product line. With Dad it was almost a religion that ideas for improving the product line should come from customers. . . .

The task force studied the magnetic tape issue for three months. When they came back, their answer was that punch cards were the best thing in the world for accounting jobs, and that magnetic tape had no place in IBM. I tried again, bringing in top salesmen and describing what magnetic tape could do, but they all ended up saying no, it's better to use punch cards.

I was beginning to learn that the majority, even the majority of top performers, are never the ones to ask when you need to make a move. You've got to feel what's going on in the world and then make the move yourself. It's pretty visceral. I didn't trust myself enough yet to insist, but I knew in my gut that we had to get into computers and magnetic tape.[1]

Having bested Remington Rand by 1956 with its mainframes, IBM promptly began to drowse again. In 1963, as he struggled to wake it up with the System/360 launch, Watson, Jr., issued this memo on bureaucracy to his subordinates.

MANAGEMENT BRIEFING
Number 6-63: October 2, 1963

TO ALL IBM MANAGERS:

I am becoming more and more concerned with the "creeping paralysis" in decision-making in IBM. We're not as fast on our feet as we should be. We often respond too slowly to the challenges and opportunities of our growing industry.

The reason for this is not that we don't have a fine corps of managers. I think we have the best in the world. The reason is that too many managers are not using all the authority that has been delegated to them.

There seems to be entirely too much double checking, too much "group-think," too many committee decisions, too many levels of approval before a proposal can be translated into action. I suspect there is probably as much "selling" effort inside IBM, among ourselves, as there is out in the field with customers.

From now on, I would like each of you to make as many decisions as you can on your own and reduce to the lowest possible level the amount of consultation, concurrence and approval involved.

I am not asking you to throw all caution to the winds and end up as dead heroes. But I am asking you to think more about getting the job done quickly, and with a minimum of "playing it safe." Every time you think about getting approval or concurrence, instead, ask yourself, "Can I make this decision here and now, on my own?"

We are moving in fast company these days, and we simply have to move faster than anyone else if we want to lead the race.[2]


System/360 proved to be the best information technology product of its time and was replaced by the even better System/370. But the bureaucracy beast continued to lurk in the undergrowth. In early 1972, when economic recession seemed to be a threat to the firm's steady expansion, then chief executive T. Vincent Learson found it necessary first to write to the management team and then to bypass them and communicate directly with employees about the problem. He turned to *Think,* IBM's internal employee magazine, to address the bureaucracy issue.


Months ago I sent out a Management Briefing to condemn a principle feature of bureaucracy—the tendency of some in IBM to pass the buck, play it safe, run from risks. But today we have still too many organizational procedures, still too many safeguards to keep people out of trouble, still too much refusal to delegate, still too much group thinking—the kind that almost never produces brilliant insight or [decisive] action. . . .

One of our top facility managers recently told me that no subject of any consequence could come up in his location without somebody's calling a meeting and having 30 people show up. His observation in itself proves his inability to correct this problem. Another IBMer wrote to me, almost in despair, of his concern—middle management has no conviction—and ended his letter, "Mr. Learson, maybe our company is too big to be productive. I sometimes yearn for the days when we were innovative and responsive to customer needs."

I'm seriously disturbed by the signs of bureaucracy, especially in times like these. And I'm delighted that people are calling a halt. Here is an assurance I want to give you: In this new year, I'm going to do all I can to fight this problem.[3]

A similar note was written almost a decade later, in 1981, by then CEO John Opel; again recession was a proximate cause, but Opel was also facing the twin threats of an unsuccessful minicomputer effort and the threat of the emerging personal computer, with which IBM was only just beginning to grapple.

MANAGEMENT BRIEFING
Number 1-81: September 11, 1981

TO ALL IBM MANAGERS:

Organizations seem to have an irresistible tendency to codify successful practices in rules, instructions and controls which soon begin to take the place of judgment. When that happens, the result is bureaucracy.

IBM is not immune. Earlier this year, reports from many sources indicated to me that a growing bureaucracy is affecting the performance of our business. . . . One study found that a development group had to wait eight weeks and get 31 signatures in order to buy a small piece of equipment needed to work on a critical business problem. People also complained that procedural roadblocks prevent them from getting the IBM equipment needed to do their jobs.

We have taken some immediate steps to introduce more common sense and flexibility in such areas as travel guidelines, employee recognition, reimbursement of expenses and approvals for meetings. We also have taken action to give additional current-line information systems equipment to our people. . . .

But such actions alone will not stop the drift toward bureaucracy. We will succeed in that effort only if you managers, at every level of the business, are willing to stand and fight bureaucracy wherever you find it. Certainly, there are policies, rules and controls that are necessary, but rules should not become a pervasive substitute for human judgment. . . .

You are managers because you've shown you have the judgment to decide what is right. I intend for you also to have the flexibility to *do* what's right.[4]

## A CYCLE OF BUREAUCRACY AND INNOVATION

IBM's history can be seen as a cycle in which innovation repeatedly gives way to bureaucracy, which is in turn broken by bold managerial action that enables innovation to flourish again.

At cycle's peak, the firm churns out market-dominating products and expands its physical plant and employment. Once past this peak, however, IBM yields to a paradox of success. Ideally, the profit surge following innovation should boost competitiveness by providing still more funds for research and development, turning IBM into a business that moves from strength to strength. In fact, adding scale as a result of marketplace success makes IBM sleepy instead. Its leaders, perhaps content to rest on their laurels or fearing the antitrust implications of too much success, begin to focus more on the minutia of administration than on the worries of their customers; as they do so, IBM's presence at the forefront slowly fades.

Only after the bottom of the cycle is reached, when the bureaucracy is at its peak and the firm's future looks grim, does IBM shake itself awake, usually at the prodding of a new chief executive. Once aroused, the firm proceeds to make the long climb back to the heights of innovation and prosperity.

To date, IBM has gone through four cycles of innovation and bureaucracy. Four times IBM has achieved dominance in the information-technology market; first with tabulators; then with early mainframe computers; then with its integrated mainframe systems; and finally with early personal computers. Four times IBM has lost market dominance as its version of the standard technology of the day passed its prime and next-generation products became mired in internal dissension. What should we make of the fact that IBM has gone through previous periods of crisis and recovery?

One obvious point is that while IBM's recent troubles are serious, they are not unique in the firm's experience. Clearly, any appearance of invincibility at IBM is an illusion. Information technology is a high-stakes game with plenty of pitfalls—even for market leaders—and media pundits and stock market analysts alike must learn to avoid ascribing "hero" or "goat" status to IBM's executives based on short-term results. When IBM is attuned to its customers, it can lead its industry; when it is mired in procedure, it falls back into the pack.

A second point is that IBM's troubles are not the result of demographics or personalities but of administrative processes. IBM was a young company in the 1980s; most of its major business units were being run by people under forty years of age—none by a person over fifty. If rigid thinking and entrenched attitudes were problems, their source probably lay not in individuals but in the system of management and culture. In recent years, IBM's culture has been very inbred: The firm hired few, if any, managers from the outside; it made no use of external university executive education programs; and its managerial mantra was "not invented here." These are fixable, not fatal, problems.

The third, and most important, point is that IBM now appears to be passing the trough of its fifth cycle. Energy and imagination are returning to the company's ranks; sluggishness, self-absorption, and delay are departing. This pattern of resurgence after decline, a very unusual achievement in the computer industry, has permitted the firm to change basic technologies and products several times. Few other information-technology firms have been able to do so even once.

When IBM scrapped tabulators for computers in the 1950s, its leading competitor was Sperry Rand. It took nearly ten years (from 1947 to 1956) for Thomas J. Watson, Jr., to get IBM to abandon tabulators and adopt the mainframe computer as its product standard, while Sperry Rand was forging ahead with the UNIVAC. Today Sperry Rand has ceased to exist as a separate company.

It took nearly ten years (from 1959 to 1967) for IBM to establish the System/360. When IBM finally made the leap, its key rivals were RCA, GE, Burroughs, Univac (a renamed Sperry Rand), NCR, Control Data, and Honeywell. Of these firms, only Control Data still makes mainframes; Burroughs (now part of Unisys) and NCR (part of AT&T) disappeared through mergers; RCA, GE, and Honeywell effectively left the information-technology industry years ago.

IBM's minicomputer effort languished from 1974 through the early 1980s while the Digital Equipment Corporation, Prime, and Data General (DG) grabbed an early lead. Today, IBM boasts the best-selling minicomputer (the AS 400), while DG is struggling and DEC is crippled.

In the most recent field of battle, distributed computing based on microcomputer networks, the fight to control market standards got started in the mid-1980s; ten years later the market positions of the leading firms are starting to build. IBM's major competitors for this market are Compaq, Dell, Apple, Microsoft, and Intel. The jury is still out on what company, if any, will control this architecture, but IBM is a player.

History thus makes it clear that IBM's greatest challenger is not a specific competitor but its own bureaucratic behavior. Insularity of viewpoint; wishful thinking and an unwillingness to recognize in a timely fashion marketplace changes; arrogance based on past successes—these are the causes of the wounds that IBM has inflicted on itself.

But why is IBM's history marked with this pattern of falling into bureaucratic lethargy and then waking up to terrorize its competitors? The answer may be found in human nature and the inertia spawned in the rapid growth of large organizations. The decision to deliberately abandon an aging but still-successful technology is hard for key executives to make because so many thousands of lives (including their own) are built on routines derived from such technologies. A new technology requires new engineering knowledge, production methods, and sales pitches; most importantly, it requires the abandonment of past success in a process akin to cannibalism. A new technology leads to turbulence and uncertainty: No one can predict whether it will sell to an established base of customers or to new ones until the sales representatives are pitching it and careers are on the line. Only when an old technology has clearly reached the end of the road does the panic to survive overcome the inertia of past practice, and executives (or their replacements) finally begin to move forward again.

In retrospect, it is easy to see why incumbent senior management might be lulled by the rhythm of established practice. It seems risky to mess with success. But the information-technology business *requires* taking large risks. Such gambles cannot be executed if the management team is preoccupied with cost cutting.

No IBM chief executive has chosen large-scale layoffs as a solution to IBM's bureaucracy problem, perhaps recognizing that the challenge was one of attitude rather than body counts. The solution to the problem of bureaucratic attitudes is to challenge and mobilize the organization with a bold vision of the future. Jobs have always flowed out of new product development at IBM.

## UNDERSTANDING THE PROCESSES OF GROWTH AND DECLINE

Businesses, like individuals, follow a life cycle. They begin as small entities endowed with few resources beyond entrepreneurial vigor, and much of their early history is an unending struggle to grow. As they find customers and evade competitors, they build capital and add people, becoming mature market leaders. Maturity, however, contains the seeds of decline: As the press of competition fades, mature firms develop the hallmarks of bureaucracy—an addiction to established practices and a rejection of innovative ideas. As younger competitors introduce new ideas, the mature firm begins to decline.

The basic assumption of the life-cycle view of business enterprises is that the cycle unfolds *despite* the firm's freedom to change any and all of its practices at any time. In theory, any firm should be immortal—it need only copy the innovations it sees around it to remain competitive. But as economic historians have repeatedly observed, this does not seem to occur; even firms that are free to change seem to fall victim to bureaucracy and then fail under the challenge of more vigorous rivals.[5]

In contrast, a model based on cycles of growth and decline finds both innovation and bureaucracy recurring inside the same organization. Properly managed, a firm with such a cycle could become perpetually renewing, although its track over time would resemble that of a roller coaster. Energy from past innovation would lift the firm toward new heights even as forward momentum was being eroded by the gradual drift toward bureaucracy. Ascendance of the bureaucracy would lead to a downward slide until management could scrap failing technologies and procedures in a fresh burst of innovation. Residual momentum would allow the low point of scale in the new cycle to remain above the low point of scale in the previous cycle. Using this model, IBM's cycles of growth and decline are depicted in Figure 3.1.

The notion of cycles of growth and decline provides a lens through which to view IBM's history and to chart its likely path forward. In this context, the true magnitude of the present crisis at IBM becomes apparent. Previous crises at IBM have all resulted in the firm's laying the base for greater scale and scope to follow; the current period of crisis seems to be the first in IBM's history in which the low point of the new cycle will fall below the low point of the previous cycle. Projecting this onto Figure 3.1 would show the dip from 1983 to 1988 bottoming out at the same low point established in the 1959–63 crisis.

For the first time in many decades, IBM will shrink as it enters a new era: Already it has cut half of its employees and lost several billion dollars in annual sales revenue from its 1991 peak of $65 billion. This loss of scale has occurred because the current shift to a client-server or networked market standard has taken place more rapidly than antici-

*Figure 3.1*   IBM's Growth and Decline as a Succession of Cycles

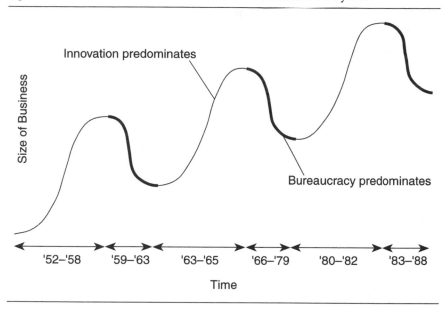

pated. But however painful the crisis of the early 1990s has been to IBM and its shareholders, it is probably only a temporary loss of position. A firm that has retained upward of $60 billion in revenues and more than 200,000 employees—even in the throes of deep internal and external turmoil—remains well above critical scale for the computer industry. All that has been lacking to trigger a new upward trend is the spark to ignite a fresh burst of innovation.

## HOW COMMITMENT TO THE CUSTOMER HAS RESCUED IBM

Many firms in the information-technology industry have been one-hit wonders. They have ridden a single product or technology to prominence and then faded from view when it was supplanted by the advances of others. Recent examples include Visi-Calc (the personal computer spreadsheet pioneer), Ashton-Tate, Burroughs, Amdahl, Wang, Data General, and now possibly DEC. From the perspective of growth and decline cycles, each of these firms moved through one full cycle ending in failure. How has IBM avoided the same fate?

IBM's fundamental commitment to customer service, based on the decision of Watson, Sr., to rent rather than sell tabulating equipment and to use rented machines as a pipeline through which to push the supplies and service that earned IBM its real profits, has kept IBM from the fate of its rivals. Commitment to customers has subordinated technology to marketing, and good marketing has always meant truly superior service—not necessarily superior equipment. IBM's key customers have always been prepared to accept slightly less than state-of-the-art technology in exchange for greater reliability and IBM's famous service package. It is thus no accident that real breakthroughs in information technology have tended to occur elsewhere than at IBM, even though IBM has the largest R&D budget in the industry.

Smaller firms simply do not have IBM's major market position or service reputation to protect them and so are more willing to gamble on leading-edge products that may still contain the occasional bug. IBM, much less willing to ruin its reputation with unreliable equipment, has thus many times found itself playing technology catch-up. It has always been able to do so because it is like a compass pointed toward its customers; whenever a breakthrough blows IBM off course by changing the marketplace, it can listen to its key accounts and reorient itself. T.J. Watson, Jr., has noted the pattern.

> In the history of IBM, technological innovation often wasn't the thing that made us successful. Unhappily there were many times when we came in second. But technology turned out to be less important than sales and distribution methods. Starting with UNIVAC, we consistently outsold people who had better technology because we knew how to put the story before the customer, how to install the machines successfully, and how to hang on to customers once we had them.[6]

IBM has thus never become fatally attached to a single technology in its entire history—despite the dogged resistance of old technology champions at each of the crises the company has confronted.

## A TEST OF THE CYCLES APPROACH TO IBM's HISTORY

Closing this chapter is a test of the validity of the cycles approach to IBM's history. Five quotations about IBM drawn from the business press are reproduced below. The reader is invited to identify the year in which each was written. Answers appear in the endnotes. Good luck!

## Quotation 1

Over the last ten years, International Business Machines has had the most impeccable of growth records. . . . Unlike any other company in computers, and almost any in other fields, its growth in sales (300% to over $3.5 billion) has been good, that in pre-tax profits even better (425%), and in dividends paid out (837%) best of all. Profit margins on sales have actually widened in the past ten years of 20 to 27% pre-tax. . . .

It requires some nerve to say that all is less than perfect in such a garden, but it may be. IBM staked a great deal of money on its new [computers]. It spent $1,150 million last year on new plant and facilities, especially for the mass production of the units used for the solid logic technology of the [new machines]. Yet it has not been able to produce units fast enough. At the same time . . . the next stage in computer development, look[s] likely to hit the scene earlier than IBM might have hoped when it planned the [new machine].[7]

## Quotation 2

In just three years International Business Machines Corp. ran through some $4 billion in cash and then borrowed $1 billion in the first bond offering of its history. It announced products it couldn't deliver, and delivered products it couldn't support with necessary services and software. . . . So, the old story. The young champion has become tired, overweight and outclassed by a host of hungry newcomers. . . . But don't bet on IBM's decline. . . .

Take a short view of the situation and you make a case that IBM is in trouble. But that is to ignore IBM's counterattack. "You can't run this business like the long-term business it is," [IBM's chairman] emphasizes, "five- or six-year product cycles, on the basis of quarter-to-quarter earnings comparisons." . . .

IBM understands very well the value of controlling the standards and still has the market clout to achieve that control. Note carefully where all this is leading. . . . IBM is doing what it has done for generations— letting a market develop until its direction is clear before letting out a steamroller carefully, very carefully, designed to flatten everything in sight. It's just that this time it's on a really grand scale—too grand, perhaps, for investors to comprehend.[8]

## Quotation 3

The decision by the management of the International Business Machines Corp. to produce a new family of computers . . . has emerged as the most crucial and portentous—as well as perhaps the riskiest—business judgment of modern times. The decision committed IBM to laying out money in sums that read like the federal budget—some $5 billion over . . . four years. . . .

The new [technology is] intended to obsolete virtually all other existing computers—including those being offered by IBM itself. . . . It [is] roughly as though General Motors had decided to scrap its existing makes and models and offer in their place one new line of cars, covering the entire spectrum of demand, with a radically redesigned engine and an exotic fuel.[9]

## Quotation 4

International Business Machines Corp. has long enjoyed a reputation as one of the world's best-run businesses. But that image has taken quite a beating over the sixteen months since IBM announced its [new machines]. . . . Within three weeks of the announcement of the new line . . . the company was deluged with orders for some 42,000 machines, more than twice as many as it planned to manufacture over the entire life of the series. . . .

Whether IBM got into trouble mainly because it under priced [its new computer] is a subject of almost metaphysical debate, even inside the company. But the trouble was brewing well before that pricing decision. For a combination of economic, technological, and competitive reasons, IBM has less control of the marketplace that it once had and less ability to predict customers' behavior. . . .

[A]s IBM tries to become fully competitive once more . . . the turmoil in the marketplace will doubtless give the company more unpleasant surprises. It will be a long time before Mother Blue's customers and investors can relax.[10]

## Quotation 5

It is indeed fortunate that [IBM's CEO] had the foresight and fortitude to gradually relax his authority during his [tenure] and permit a youthful, self-reliant executive team to develop. For though the company is now at the very peak of its power and profitability, it is also at a critical crossroads in its business life where large decisions, from which there is no returning, have to be made. . . .

The fact is that the once impregnable IBM Corp. has become a target—a target not just for legal actions but for legitimate competitors, large and small, who can now move in more quickly and effectively on IBM's pastures than they have been able to in the past. In spite of the new antitrust rules, it is doubtful if any competitor will do much more than dent IBM's entrenched position in [established products]. But the new field . . . is wide open.[11]

# IBM's Megastrategy

# A Single Face to the Customer

Unlike most other firms, IBM has had for many years not only a business strategy but also a megastrategy—the firm's top executives worked to coordinate the narrower visions and product offerings of the various business units according to a broader, two-pronged managerial purpose based on an approach to customers and an approach to employees.

For its customers, IBM sought to be a single source for all of their information technology shopping; for its employees, IBM sought to be like a family, providing security and fair treatment in return for loyalty and top performance. IBM's methods for establishing employee loyalty, the subject of the next chapter, were not unique, but its efforts went beyond those of most other American companies. The single-source concept—or singleness—was unique to IBM: It was the only competitor in the information technology industry to stick to this approach through thick and thin. How did IBM conceive and implement singleness and how well has this strategy served the company?

## THE IMPORTANCE OF RENTALS

IBM's most basic business objective has always been to maintain a long-term presence in an industry characterized by rapid, constant, and substantial change. Founder T. J. Watson, Sr., understood that a long-term presence in information technology meant creating a service business, not a technology business. How did he develop this perspective?

Watson, Sr., controlled IBM at a time when business machines were rented, not purchased. Information technology users did not want to sink capital into equipment that—even in the 1910s–1920s—tended to become obsolete relatively quickly. Information technology vendors made their real profits from selling supplies and providing repair services, and they considered themselves lucky if the stream of rental payments on a machine covered the costs of engineering and building its replacement. In other words, the machine was only a conduit through which business was conducted.

Needing to accumulate billions of dollars' worth of machines in inventory, IBM found itself in a delicate position. If a customer were to become disenchanted with IBM's level of service or degree of commitment, it could simply cancel its rental agreements and force IBM to retrieve its property. These machines would then stop earning their keep, becoming a disposal headache for IBM. Fear of these developments drove Watson, Sr., to keep IBM's people focused on customer service, driving this objective into IBM's cultural values—particularly its values of excellence in execution and best customer service.[1]

To maximize its ability to deliver customer service, IBM developed the megastrategy described above. *Singleness,* providing one-stop shopping for information-technology customers, was coupled with policies ensuring that specific employees—IBM's face to the customer—both remained loyal to their employer and were motivated to put the customer first.

## WHAT IS SINGLENESS?

IBM has always considered itself to be one business—trying to meet all of the needs of its key customers for better, faster, and cheaper information-technology systems and services. Singleness thus strives to be all things to some people, to provide complete information-management systems for select business customers. Singleness should thus be distinguished from *vertical integration, synergy,* and a *niche strategy.*

Singleness targets the external marketplace, implying that the firm will provide a full range of products and services to its customers.

Vertical integration deals with the internal structure of a firm; it is the locking together of buyers and suppliers through contracts, alliances, or mergers to create more efficient production, distribution, marketing, or administration, the savings from which may or may not be shared with customers. A PC firm that practices vertically integrated manufacturing, for example, would probably both make and assemble key components such as processors or memory chips; one that does not would either make a component (as Intel does) or assemble components into computers (as Compaq does). A company can embrace singleness without being vertically integrated and vice versa. For example, Bloomingdale's tries to fulfill all the apparel, accessory, and furnishing needs of its upscale customers and yet designs and manufactures very little, if any, of the merchandise it sells. Levi Strauss, on the other hand, designs and manufactures much of its apparel but does not try to satisfy the entire clothing needs of its targeted customers.

IBM has used both singleness and vertical integration in recent decades, and many apparent criticisms of IBM's singleness are really criticisms of its excessive vertical integration. Analysts and customers typically do not fault IBM for trying to provide entire computer systems; rather, they cite high costs, which are often the result of seeking too much control over the supply chain instead of relying on market forces to keep suppliers in line.

Singleness differs from synergy in that where singleness is externally focused, synergy describes internal interactions among the parts of a broader whole that generate value for a customer. Does achieving effective singleness require IBM's business units to generate synergy? Yes. One example of this process in action is the symbiotic relationship among the three IBM units that market mainframes, operating systems, and database products. IBM's DB/2 was a late entrant into a crowded market, and yet it has now become the premier mainframe database product. IBM achieved this partly by designing specific enhancements into successive generations of mainframes and operating systems to improve DB/2's performance. Increased DB/2 usage has, in turn, generated demand for additional hardware.

IBM's singleness strategy also differs distinctly from a niche strategy. A niche strategy is typically used by a small company to focus on a corner of a market that larger players have neglected. This neglect may have come about for various reasons: the technology involved may not yet be mature enough to risk commercialization; the cost structures of the leading firms may be too high to make the undertaking profitable; or the potential profits in the niche may be deemed too small or uncertain to meet investment requirements.

Many firms looking to enter the information-technology market pursue niche strategies. The reason is the sheer scale of investment required to embrace singleness; IBM must continually invest billions of dollars in new technology to maintain a full line of products and services. Firms successfully lodged in a niche, like Microsoft, with its PC operating systems and applications software, must still shell out many millions, but their overall scale of investment is far less than IBM's.

There are several risks in a niche strategy to set against its lessened financial burden. Unable to offer a full range of information-technology products and services, a niche player cannot reap the superior profits that providers of fully integrated solutions earn; it must rely on others to provide the pieces of systems which it cannot. In addition, niche competitors that fail to branch out have much less protection against changing technology standards than do companies with positions in multiple niches. Only so-called full-service providers can truly dominate information technology and reap the profits of a market leader. Although IBM uses niche strategies, it is not a true niche player because its business units strive to tie their products and services together.

Trying to pursue singleness in a rapidly changing marketplace has some disadvantages. If a major technology transition comes along affecting only one part of the product line, for example, the entire firm must still change in response. To avoid this, many large firms decentralize, spreading their bets on products and services. When a decision to change direction—to cannibalize existing technologies—is eventually made, however, a single company can implement it with relative speed and dispatch. Managers in such firms are accustomed to thinking about the entire business—not just one piece of it—and the systems to make a coordinated change are all in place.

In the information-technology industry, in which there are thousands of firms pursuing niche strategies, the odds are high that a few will find success. In an era when uncertainty over computing's ultimate direction allows technology to dominate marketing, a few niche players even come to control some market segments. The real question is whether this situation will become permanent. IBM's singleness approach has served it well in the past by limiting competitors to niches and by steadily eroding the niches as each generation of technology matured.

## SHOULD SINGLENESS BE ABANDONED?

Many observers have argued that IBM should split itself up to give its business units autonomy and free rein in a shifting market. Some have suggested IBM should become a holding company; others have suggested that its units become independent companies, each with its own stockholders. In any case, if IBM were broken up, singleness would be impossible.

Arguments that singleness is outdated are based on dramatic changes in IBM's customers. Purchasing managers or general executives now make the computer purchase decisions once made by information-technology experts. Managers can put together cost-effective systems, it is argued, by buying components from many different suppliers. Despite their relative lack of expertise, these managers are nonetheless able to make informed judgments about assembling information systems because they hire on consultants to assist them. The consultants in a sense substitute for one-stop shopping from a vendor like IBM. The customers no longer need a single-source supplier, and if they don't need one, they certainly aren't going to pay a premium to have one. From this perspective, there is no marketplace advantage to singleness, and IBM should give it up.

But is abandoning singleness and breaking up IBM, in fact, best for the company?

Separation of business units makes sense where there is no need for extensive coordination and interaction among business units occupying different markets. IBM, on the other hand, is essentially in one business. Thomas J. Watson, Sr., stated long ago that IBM was in the business of meeting its customers' needs for information processing, and in the mid-1990s, it is still doing just exactly that. The size and complexity of information technology may have changed over the years, but its essence remains much the same.

Today, as in the past, IBM faces competitors staking out major niches. What would distinguish a newly independent IBM business unit from its competitors? Not much, other than the IBM brand name. Independent business units will not necessarily have more capital, better research and development, leaner manufacturing, or superior marketing than do their niche competitors. How then can IBM compete in an industry full of niche competitors who know their niches as well as, if not better than, IBM does? The answer lies in the needs of customers for smoothly integrated and functioning information systems—exactly IBM's traditional strength. IBM's ability to respond to its customers' total information service needs, the trait that has distinguished it and allowed it to rise above its niche competitors, would vanish with fragmentation.

During Frank Cary's tenure as chief executive, IBM attempted to split into a division focusing on big systems and another focused on small systems. The two divisions ended up trying to market to the same customers, and the result was loss of focus in the company and confusion among its customers, many of whom seemed to prefer an IBM that presented a single face. This experience helps to explain why even though IBM has the option to decentralize, it doesn't do so. Unlike large decentralized firms such as General Electric and Johnson & Johnson, IBM has potential synergies among its units. Only some form of centralized management structure allows exploitation of these synergies. Such centralization needn't mean that IBM units have no autonomy or discretion, but it does imply more central direction than prevails in firms with diverse businesses.

A final reason why IBM has not wanted to abandon singleness can be found in the ongoing evolution of the information-technology industry. For many years, large-scale firms offering proprietary solutions dominated the industry. Much of this structure has been swept away by the move to open systems, a move sparked by IBM itself when it gave away control over the personal computer architecture to outsiders Intel and Microsoft, and leaving the door open for Compaq and other clone manufacturers.

For a decade or more, the chaos and confusion of open systems have been taken as normal, and even as desirable—a throwing-off of the shackles of conformity imposed on the world by "Big Brother–Big Blue." Unfortunately for the niche players like Microsoft, Apple, or

Intel, who have so greatly benefited from open systems, information technology is unlikely to remain fragmented. Major buyers of computer systems will not spend enormous sums to pull together into functioning systems the divergent technologies pursued by vendors for computer chips, software, operating systems, and networking software. Neither a Microsoft nor an Intel, perched as they are at the front and in the middle of the information-technology value chain, can maintain control over the full array of market standards embodied in the microcomputer. Intel microprocessors must be built into vendor platforms, and Microsoft operating systems and applications must have a host on which to run. Neither firm acting alone can provide integrated solutions as IBM can. This issue promises to become more important as the microcomputer and related networking technologies mature and buyers again consider marketing and service along with pure price and functionality in their technology purchases.

After a decade in which companies took advantage of price competition among vendors by buying components—and paid a post-purchase price in integration headaches—single-source solutions are beginning to look more attractive again. Why would a customer looking to buy several thousand personal computer network nodes absorb the headaches of dealing with multiple vendors, as is the implication of an open-systems marketplace, when it could look for a single-source solution—information technology developed by one vendor? The answer may well be that it will do the latter, opening an opportunity for IBM.

While it seems clear that IBM will not enjoy the margins that it once did on proprietary mainframes, it is likely that some measure of its former competitiveness will be restored as the industry re-integrates and the value of the single-source solution reappears. Singleness continues to have a large potential reward.

# The Loyalty System

T HROUGH ITS megastrategy—based on the two pillars, singleness and loyalty—IBM has traditionally linked its marketing and sales strategy directly to its human resources strategy. IBM's well-thought-out approach—rooted in values, articulated in an unwritten social contract, and expressed in specific policies and practices—was designed to create and maintain employee loyalty.

Loyalty at IBM was two-sided: The company was loyal to the employee and the employee to the company. Going far beyond a no-layoff principle, management established a number of policies to encourage employee trust and pride in IBM. Trusting and proud, they made excellent representatives of the firm, and lifelong IBMers forged enduring bonds with customers. For the company, employee loyalty, much more than a feel-good objective, was the means to a greater end—the sustained competitiveness of IBM.

Responding to the promises of its loyalty contract, people who wanted to work in the information-technology industry and who had a high personal need for security came in droves to IBM. IBM's social contract was well known in the industry, and especially within IBM; a random sample survey of IBM's employees in the mid-1980s showed that fully 97 percent of the company's employees were well acquainted with the firm's full-employment practice and more than 90 percent of those said the practice was very important to them. From the 1950s through the 1980s, employees knew that IBM did not promise job security, but employment security; employees were expected to be flexible about retraining, reassignment, and relocation, if necessary. IBMers accepted this, and in turn expected the company to keep its promise to them.

Managers debate the question of whether employment security enhances or lessens employee motivation, with ample arguments and examples available on both sides. Asking employees if they respond best to security or insecurity yields a similar range of responses. Over many years, we have often asked groups of people the following question: "On the whole, do you do your best work when you feel secure in your job or when there is a danger of losing it?" Some will respond, "I do my best work when I can concentrate on my tasks without being distracted by fear of losing my job"; others say "I do my best work when I'm under pressure and I know that if I don't succeed, I'll suffer some serious penalty, like losing my job." In this less-than-fully-scientific survey, we have found that people in the general population divide themselves fairly evenly between motivation by security and by insecurity.

But IBMers are not the general population. A self-selected group, they had for decades sought employment with IBM because of their strong need for employment security. When the company suddenly, and with little warning, abandoned its full employment practice and began to lay off employees, a huge wave of disillusionment and concern swept through the firm, and that wave is only now beginning to crest. IBM is holding closely its employee-attitude survey data, but discussions with managers in the firm indicate that morale has declined precipitously. Some managers suggest that important employees are virtually paralyzed with concern about losing their jobs.

First articulated by T. J. Watson, Sr., in the 1920s, IBM's megastrategy did not change significantly, despite the pressures of subsequent economic ups and downs, until the early 1990s, when the company tore down the loyalty pillar. We feel strongly that this was a mistake. In our study of IBM, we've found that when IBM's management team loses sight of the founder's megastrategy, it places the firm in the greatest difficulty. Tearing down one of the pillars of this megastrategy—inadvertently or not—without having a replacement in plain sight strikes us as a risky action that rather than salvaging the company may actually compound the damage already done.

## UNDERSTANDING EMPLOYEE LOYALTY AT IBM

Loyalty in a business balances the mutual expectations of workers and managers. Workers expect reasonable compensation, certain benefits, recognition for performance, a safe and pleasant working environment, and fair treatment by managers. The firm's managers expect employee loyalty, efficient and productive work, and initiative.

How well employees and their employer bind together depends on how completely the expectations of each side are met by the other. When expectations are unfulfilled, the power of the social contract wanes; when expectations are met or exceeded, its power waxes.[1] Management at IBM, as elsewhere, thus had to give to its employees in order to receive from them.

The firm's documents show how IBM built its employee relations to reflect its basic beliefs. Late in 1965, Thomas J. Watson, Jr., then IBM's chief executive, prepared for distribution a management briefing discussing the firm's values and the policies and practices meant to implement them. Watson included these paragraphs on employees.

IBM seeks to provide a maximum degree of satisfaction on the part of its employees in their assigned tasks. This is accomplished by recognition and utilization of their abilities as well as by the development of team spirit and good morale through understanding of the individual employee's attitudes, ambitions, problems, and desires. IBM's basic precept is respect of the rights and dignity of the individual. In order to contribute fully toward the accomplishment of this principle, there are provided:

- Equitable compensation in relation to skill, responsibility, and performance.
- Promotion in accordance with merit.
- Opportunities for training, study, and self-improvement.
- Protection towards illness, disability, retirement, and death.
- Safe, clean working space in pleasant surroundings.
- Effective two-way communication between management and employees.

In return, IBM expects its employees to give their loyalty and their sincere best efforts toward furthering the interests of the company. We must all

work together for the benefit of the company and the people who constitute IBM.[2]

Clearly, the megastrategy of loyalty and singleness was designed to
further the company's three basic values: the pursuit of excellence,
the best customer service, and respect for employees. The third value,
of course, is key to the other two: Excellence and the best service, in
the eyes of the customer, are in the hands of IBM's employees to
deliver. IBM therefore sought to treat its employees in a generous
fashion, so that they would treat IBM's customers in an outstanding
fashion. Management's respect for the individual employee was thus
transformed by employees into excellence in execution and the best
service for customers.

### Management's Respect for the Individual

Meritocracy permeated all of IBM's personnel policies. The classic
example is the firm's hiring practices. T. J. Watson, Sr., insisted on
recruiting the best people he could find—even if this meant ignoring
the discrimination widespread in his day. This helps to explain why
IBM had international employees in U.S. locations in the 1920s, female
technicians in the 1930s, and black professionals in the 1940s—many
years before other leading firms made similarly unbiased hiring decisions.

IBM consistently tried to hire the best in part because it was the
only way to deny competitors the talent they needed to serve IBM
customers better than IBM itself could. Talent simply could not be
allowed to go elsewhere—such was the highly competitive nature of
a service business.

IBM's policy on diversity was bluntly articulated by Tom Watson,
Jr., in 1953.

> It is the policy of this organization to hire people who have the personal-
> ity, talent and background necessary to fill a given job, regardless of race,
> color or creed.
> If everyone in IBM who hires new employees will observe this rule, the
> corporation will obtain the type of people it requires, and at the same
> time we will be affording an equal opportunity to all in accordance with
> American tradition.[3]

Employee involvement became a standard practice in IBM long before it became a management buzzword in the 1980s, and it was routinely applied to some of the most sensitive areas of the business. Watson, Sr., for example, structured IBM's sales force so that individuals and, later, account teams had exclusive territories.

Exclusivity offered many benefits as a management technique. It curbed infighting over who would get larger and more lucrative accounts—once assigned, these accounts stayed with a particular representative until performance no longer justified the assignment. It supported the direct measurement of sales performance: If a territory yielded higher or lower sales than planned, responsibility was not diluted by overlapping "ownership." It let representatives form the strong relationships that IBM required to sustain a service business. Most importantly, exclusivity clearly conveyed to representatives that their managers trusted them. IBM's sales representatives, *and no one else,* represented IBM to their accounts; if a customer had a problem, the sales representative could expect a message from the customer and was duty-bound to respond.

In some firms, sales staff could not be trusted with the power of account exclusivity; should a representative have a dispute with the firm's management, he or she would have the leverage to take the account elsewhere or seriously weaken the relationship. That Watson, Sr., was willing to take this risk was a hallmark of his belief in the power of values; he trusted that no IBM salesperson would do such a thing to an IBM customer.

Employee involvement was also reinforced through a powerful grievance procedure—the Open Door. The Open Door concept derived from the beliefs and practices of Watson, Sr. Fundamentally a hands-on manager, his door was always open so that he could hear the concerns and suggestions of employees. As IBM grew and it became impractical for employees to visit him personally, Watson, Sr., established the Open Door program to provide a means through which employees could write to him; in turn, Watson, Sr., pledged that he, and later his executive assistants, would investigate the concerns raised and— regardless of outcome—write back. Many of IBM's top executives underwent leadership tests by spending a year resolving Open Door grievances. Watson, Sr., viewed these experiences as one true test of effective management under fire.

The most important effect of the Open Door policy was to ensure that IBM managers listened to subordinates before taking action. Although managers always held full formal authority—IBM operated as a top-down hierarchy—they used that authority under risk of review from above if prompted by employee complaints. When taken in conjunction with IBM's full employment practice, the Open Door became a serious weapon in employees' hands. People had little compunction about voicing their opinions when they spotted improprieties, since they were protected when doing so.

IBM also created a system to involve those without complaints to make. IBM employees are asked to complete anonymous questionnaires on IBM policy and practices at least once each year. The survey yields standardized data that can be aggregated by unit or function to show trends in employee concerns.

IBM turned the notion of a safe and healthy workplace into one of the most comprehensive benefit plans ever seen. One company publication described the three goals of the program.

> IBM's employee benefits and services programs are . . . designed to offer *protection* against temporary loss of income and medical expenses due to sickness or accident, *security* through retirement, capital accumulation, disability income and death benefits and *opportunity* through educational assistance, vacation and holidays.[4]

IBM offered a comprehensive medical care program that included sickness and accident income supplements, travel accident insurance, the employee assistance program (EAP), an IBM health education program, and a personal health account. The pension plan included tax-deferred saving, an ESOP, and group life insurance and survivor benefits. IBM also provided bridges to retirement including pre-retirement seminars; leave programs; and technical, academic, and community service career programs. Vacation and holiday plans meted out generous time-off benefits.

IBM established a reputation as a leading force in compensation management as well. Watson, Sr., established a commission structure that made the typical IBM salesperson one of the best paid in any industry in his time, giving IBM the pick of the available sales talent. In non-sales compensation, IBM was among the market leaders, but its pay plans were better noted for their strict adherence to equity and generous benefits. No one in the firm was to be paid more (or less) than peers doing similar work elsewhere in IBM; all employees were to be paid well relative to those in other firms.

Pay equity across the firm was reinforced by the most up-to-date work evaluation schemes available and extended even to payments for superior performance. IBM merit bonuses were kept to a minimum of total pay, were doled out based on individual performance-appraisal criteria, and consisted of relatively small cumulative increments in base salary. There were no large payments to stimulate the envy of other employees or to encourage managers to play favorites among their direct reports; the only way to gain a meaningful increase in pay was to work harder than one's peers over a very long period of time. IBM used its performance-appraisal process and higher salary increases for only its best performers; long-term top performers could earn as much as 50 percent more than less effective employees in the same job.

Why so much attention to salary administration? The stated reason was to fulfill one of the company's cultural values; a more pragmatic reason was that work-group management becomes more difficult when pay for same job varies widely. Cohesion and morale suffer when people are asking why they are paid differently from their peers.

An IBM internal publication, "Everything You Wanted to Know About Pay," explains pay equity to employees.

> Maintaining salary equity is a basic management responsibility. To assist management, IBM has implemented a number of administrative procedures: job evaluation, performance planning and evaluation, salary program guidelines, second-line management review, and senior mgmt/company executive involvement in the implementation of the merit pay program. These procedures ensure that all IBM employees are given fair and equitable salary treatment. On a broader basis, other programs exist (such as the Speak-Up program, the opinion survey process and the Open Door policy) to ensure equity.
>
> Equity begins when an individual is hired. Of course, IBM adheres to all Federal laws which prohibit discrimination in hiring and salary practices with regard to race, creed, color, religion, sex, age, national origin or handicap. . . .
>
> Once on board, employees come under the merit pay system which is designed to recognize each individual's contribution to the business. All

employees are compensated consistent with their job responsibility and performance. Managers are responsible for ensuring the employees are classified into the title, code and level of the job to which they are assigned and that performance planning, counseling and evaluation [PPC&E] sessions are conducted on a timely basis.

In addition, it is each manager's responsibility to see that—when job level, time in position and length of sustained performance are similar— salary equity exists among individuals in protected groups and their peers. Managers are aided in this through periodic assessments by the Personnel Department. Peer group analyses are performed for each person in a protected group. That person's salary is compared to the average salary of peers who have the same appraisal and have been in similar job levels for a comparable period of time. These reviews highlight differences in pay which are then investigated by personnel and line management. As a result of such a review, an increase may be granted that is larger or sooner than that suggested by the Salary Guide. An adjustment of this type assures internal equity.[5]

Watson, Sr., also recognized that money alone did not motivate performance. He understood that sales representatives, often working alone much of the time, greatly valued non-material recognition from their peers as well as monetary compensation from their managers. He created week-long sales meetings at which he handed out—with enormous hoopla—relatively small awards to representatives before the assembled IBM sales force.

Finally, there was the practice of full employment, developed when IBM undertook to keep all of its employees working in the depths of the Great Depression of the 1930s. The practice later acquired a broader purpose, and managers were told not to discharge employees without cause except under the most extreme circumstances.

In an interview, Walt Burdick, former executive vice president for human resources at IBM, called full employment "the ultimate expression of respect for the individual at IBM." The practice was IBM's way of indicating that its respect for the individual was more than a homily that went no deeper than verbal assurance. IBM made this value a reality for its employees through the most tangible of all benefits that an employer can bestow on its employees: real security in their jobs.

Full employment at IBM meant that employees would not be laid off for lack of work: IBM would retrain or reassign them. And management was prepared to run the business accordingly. Exhibit 5.1 details a variety of actions to be taken by management in the event of a deterioration in the company's financial situation. The existence of this plan suggests that IBM was prepared, far in advance of any particular crisis, to handle business difficulties. The chart shows that a variety of actions have been specified, covering both financial and personnel decisions. Also significant is that in an extreme situation the burden of a loss of profitability falls both on investors—who might lose their dividends—and on employees—who might lose their jobs.

Thus Exhibit 5.1 suggests that full employment was a less firm guarantee than is often maintained; it remained contingent on performance—as defined by management. In essence, IBM could take a series of steps of graduated severity as profits turned into losses. Should the corporation ultimately find itself losing money, layoffs would be considered. IBM thus made clear to its managers that employment security was not an unqualified guarantee but was contingent on the firm's continuing financial success. It was a bargain with employees—employment security for top performance. If performance lagged, then employment security might have to go.

### Employee Performance

In return for full employment, employees had to be adaptable and flexible in their careers. Full employment practices never meant that IBMers could keep the same job during all their years with the firm. What the company guaranteed was not the employee's specific job assignment, but employment with the firm—not job security, but employment security.

IBM executives understood that in a rapidly changing industry such as information technology, many jobs would disappear each year, but they also knew that in a successful firm new jobs would take their places. Management guaranteed that IBMers would get those jobs—via transfers and retraining. This then was the essence of the social contract at IBM: employment security for the employee and loyalty and top performance for the company.

To make the full-employment promise function, the firm's Performance Planning, Contribution, and Evaluation system (PPC&E) was instituted. PPC&E was an objective-setting and appraisal process in which employees met with managers to set work objectives and discuss

*Exhibit 5.1* Management's Potential Actions to Protect Full Employment

| | Increasing Severity of Business Difficulty | | | |
|---|---|---|---|---|
| | Competitive pressure | Missing profit objectives | Insufficient profit/ negligible unit profit | Losses appear (corporate) |
| Financial Actions | Control/Reduce <br> ■ Unit transfers <br> ■ Consultant use <br> ■ Extensive training | Control/Reduce <br> ■ Off-site meetings <br> ■ Consultants <br> ■ Extensive training | Stop <br> ■ Off-sites <br> ■ Consultants <br> ■ Extensive training | Reduce or eliminate dividend |
| Executive Programs (permanent) | Impose program restraints | Curb all incentive increases | Suspend perks <br> Suspend awards | Reduce pay |
| Compensation Benefits | Suspend economic updates, coverage, size/timing <br><br> Suspend improving range moves, control promotions | Cap benefits (retirees) <br> Limit awards <br> Force vacations <br><br> Suspend stock purchase plan | Eliminate subsidies <br> Force vacations <br> Suspend increases <br> Eliminate nonlegal and compliance <br><br> Reduce pay (temporary) <br> Expand co-share benefits | Make benefits contributory (plus retirees) <br> Reduce pay (permanent) <br><br> Revise pension plan <br> Employees pay all benefits <br> Terminate pension plan |

| | | | | |
|---|---|---|---|---|
| Work Force Structure | Reduce nonregulars<br>Redeploy/retrain<br>Move work/people<br>Control hiring | Involuntary reassignments<br>Cut foreign assignments<br>Reduce contract employment | Eliminate nonregulars<br>Curtail all hiring<br>Facility closings | Layoffs (regular) |
| Work Time | Voluntary<br>Part-time<br>Cut overtime<br>Expand voluntary leaves of absence | Encourage<br>▪ Leaves of absence<br>▪ Time off<br>Eliminate overtime<br>▪ Voluntarily cut hours | Unpaid discretionary days<br>Reduce work week | Fixed closings (unpaid)<br>Furlough |

the criteria to be used in measuring performance. It also provided a mechanism for documenting plans and evaluations.

PPC&E was intended to ensure that dismissals and promotions in IBM met the spirit of full employment. Under PPC&E, only continuing poor performance—not managerial fiat—could lead to an employee's dismissal. Good performance—not managerial favor—could lead to an employee bonus or promotion. In an era in which favoritism by managers determined the fate of employees at many companies, PPC&E distinguished IBM's social contract from those of its peers, not only for employment security but also for fair treatment.

## IBM's PERFECTION OF THE OLD SOCIAL CONTRACT

The old social contract in America provided cradle-to-grave security for professional, managerial, and other key white-collar employees. Union-negotiated collective bargaining agreements provided blue-collar workers with employment security, including protection from layoffs based on seniority.

IBM extended the social contract for professionals and managers to cover all employees, avoiding a union contract for its blue-collar workers by providing pay and benefits comparable those in the best union contracts. IBM went even further, placing all employees, including blue-collar workers, on salary with salaried benefits and replacing seniority in layoffs with employment security for all employees. IBM employees thus had the most extensive employment security in American industry. They had the best of the old social contract.

Historically, what gave IBM the will to hold on when products became obsolete and pundits declared the company finished as a force in information technology? Its hidden source of strength was its social contract—morale could be maintained despite economic uncertainty and marketplace confusion.

## WHY IBM's SOCIAL CONTRACT WORKED SO WELL FOR SO LONG

Thomas J. Watson, Sr., with profound insight into motivation in the information-technology industry, realized that for all its focus on gadgets, the industry remained a service business. People did not want to *own* technology that rapidly went obsolete; they wanted to use it and replace it when better equipment came along. Users were prepared to pay a premium to vendors who would rent rather than sell them equipment and who would guarantee that this equipment would not break down on-site. Watson saw clearly that superior service would win the game.

Success in a service business depends on management's ability to motivate those who deliver the service; without proper delivery, service has no value. And so Watson, Sr., saw that a positive relationship with employees would be as critical to IBM's success as were its patents. This thinking led him to develop practices such as full employment rather than viewing wages as short-term expenditures to be matched to short-term business conditions. Watson would have said that he was making an investment in employees who were as real an asset to IBM as its patents and machine inventories.

Watson, Sr., had the additional great insight to recognize that in a service business, the implicit side of the social contract would be critical to profitability. This was counter-intuitive; the theory of his day was dominated by proponents of scientific management, who suggested that workers needed close supervision because they were lazy and that laziness could be cured with more pay.[6] But service firms were not manufacturers; they could not pack people into carefully defined jobs under close management observation and control. Employees of service firms worked in close proximity to customers—not managers—and they needed flexibility and scope to be able to please these customers.

No management team using the strictures of scientific management could hope to control and motivate a large work force spread across thousands of sites using diverse methods to please their customers. The firm's profits would have been buried under administrative costs had it attempted to do so. Instead, IBM had to learn to use its culture instead of pay to motivate employees; its employees had to be made to believe that *they were the firm,* and this meant using the devices of respect, recognition, and involvement.

Employee involvement and respect for the individual, as Watson, Sr., understood them, appear to present-day eyes to be highly paternalistic; in terms of understanding the relationship of human motivation to the requirements of IBM's business, however, the strategies were brilliant, and these key insights remain valid today even as IBM's management dismantles the practices in their original form.

For despite its substantial role in IBM's success over many years, IBM's social contract was always suspect in the investment community. It was said that IBM was too generous to employees and that it provided employment security because it could afford to do so. The connection between employment security and employee performance was either not perceived or disbelieved. Whenever a business crisis loomed, analysts urged the company to cut costs by laying off employees.

Until 1993, IBM refused. "Full employment is the cornerstone of employee loyalty at IBM," John Akers told a business school audience in 1992. He left unstated the implication that to remove the cornerstone might cause the entire structure to collapse. Today Akers's successors are busy chipping away at this cornerstone, with an uncertain impact on IBM's future.

## WHAT IS THE NEW SOCIAL CONTRACT?

By the early 1990s, both of the key elements of the old social contract in America were almost gone. There was no cradle-to-grave security left for managers, professionals, and key white-collar people, and union contracts protected only about one in ten private business employees.

What has replaced the old social contract? Fluidity. Companies now expect people to leave the firm, not to stay for an entire career. In the past, companies and employees expected that employees would relocate frequently over the course of a career; now many employees stay put in their homes and switch employers.

A more fluid relationship benefits firms, but also those employees who are willing to take risks. More educated, better skilled, and more traveled, these people can embrace risk because they have more opportunities and a fall-back position.

In today's new social contract, employee loyalty may be directed not toward the company but toward the employee's work team, colleagues, technology, project, or leader. This is similar to how non-profit organizations motivate their employees: They hope that people will be loyal to the mission and to their local units rather that to the national or international organization.

IBM, once the epitome of the old social contract, has been trying to make the transition to the new. The company has abandoned its full employment practice and is seeking more fluidity in its employment practices generally—IBM has even abandoned its expectation of employee loyalty. After decades of adhering to a social contract in order to gain and hold the loyalty of each IBM employee, the company has changed its objective. The connection between loyalty and performance that IBM policy once assumed has been abandoned. IBM today expects performance without loyalty.

But the firm is looking in a different direction for employee commitment that will benefit the company. A company gets only mediocre performance from uncommitted people. Recognizing that top performance is not achieved without some commitment, IBM is encouraging commitment to the work group. This is a fundamental, but largely unnoted, source of the sudden popularity of work teams in American business. Teams often work better than do supervised individuals.

Loyalty to a team can substitute for loyalty to the firm for many employees, who work better in teams because they can bond themselves to their teammates. People need to belong, if not to the firm—which has told them they are expendable—then to their work team—which often treats them as if they were members of a family.

To a person familiar with the old system, team loyalty can introduce some bizarre twists. People who distrust and even resent their companies can nonetheless be top performers because of their commitment to their work team. Logic insists that the employee will see that working to benefit the team ultimately benefits the company as well, and so will be likely to reduce commitment to the team. But so strong is the need for belonging, for the illusion if not the reality of acceptance and security, that people disregard the clear logic of the situation and perform mightily for the team even when the consequence is clearly to benefit the firm to which they are no longer loyal. IBM—like other companies—did not develop from theory the new notion of commitment as a substitute for loyalty; they didn't find it in academic journals, but stumbled across it in practice and seized upon the opportunity it offers.

The companies are often hypocritical. They say they want people to be passionate about their work, but they keep raising the level of expectation about performance and reducing the resources available.

This places continuing stress on the individual: Perform or be kicked out. Often, the company must increase demands—it may be facing challenges in the marketplace and require greater performance while having fewer resources. But even though the situation may be real—not feigned—it remains stressful to the employees involved.

## THE SPECIAL SITUATION OF MANAGERS

The changed social contract has special implications for the relationship between managers and firms. Managers used to identify with the company—in fact, they were the company. Shareholders owned it, but management controlled it. This is still the case in a certain sense, but power has shifted. Managers are less in control of the company; they have been replaced by product and capital markets.

In the past a manager might decide to accept losses in the short term to gain a long-term advantage. This is still possible, but far less likely, because investors are unwilling to tolerate losses for what may be an elusive long-term gain.

There are certain exceptions to this. If management makes a strong case to analysts that a long-term gain will result from short-term losses, investors may accept the argument. When managements take special charges against earnings (losses), the share price will sometimes nevertheless increase if investors expect the write-offs to be one time only and to set the stage for greater profits in the future.

But these are commonly recognized as exceptions to the rule, even by Wall Street defenders. In the usual situation, managers have become much more visible as information about profits and losses becomes more readily available and activist investors question management's choices when losses appear. Executives are more vulnerable to capital market discipline than they were even a few years ago; losses put their jobs on the line. Activist boards dismiss executives who fail to deliver consistent short-term profits. Executives under this pressure dismiss managers who fail to deliver results from their departments. Cradle-to-grave employment security is gone for managers and executives just as it is gone for employees generally.

This is, of course, exactly what supporters of capital market discipline want. In their view—and it has some validity—investors in the past were far too tolerant of ineffectual managers who rationalized losses as the price to be paid for future gains that never materialized. But in many cases the opposite was true. Excellent executives and managers have lost their positions for pursuing long-term gain at the expense of short-term profits. Defenders of shareholder activism might say that these were simply unfortunate, unintended consequences, the results of misunderstandings by boards of directors or investors. Nonetheless, the risk to executives is real, and many executives have concluded that the old social contract that enabled them to identify confidently their interests with those of the company is no longer valid. As a result, executives now look less to the company's and their own long-term interest and more to making quick gains which translate into their own financial advantage, and to getting out of the firm while the getting's good.

This has been the pattern at IBM. Executives and managers can no longer count on employment security, so they are pushing costs down and trying to squeeze more profit out of stagnant sales. Carried too far, this approach will mortgage the firm's future. When a technology transformation occurs, IBM must accept declining profitability for a term while it repositions itself in the marketplace—this is the essence of the industry's dynamic. As a result of the changed social contract, IBM executives are now less likely to reposition the firm effectively than they were in the past because their own long-term interests are no longer tightly tied to those of IBM.

## CHANGE—OR NO CHANGE?

An argument could be made that there has been no change in IBM's social contract. The firm had always held that employment security depended on business success: In the early 1990s, when the firm began to experience losses, it began to lay off employees. But two aspects of IBM's situation in the early 1990s make this interpretation suspect.

First, the company sustained almost no operating losses: Only a tiny portion of IBM's huge financial losses were caused by operating losses; the rest were self-inflicted restructuring charges. Second, IBM's business reversals were only partially attributable to failing performance by rank-and-file employees. First among its key failings was its relinquishment of control of the new personal computer technology to competitors, clearly top management's responsibility. A simultaneous business downturn in IBM's major international markets was also not the fault of rank-and-file IBMers. This accentuates employees' sense of betrayal: A downturn was exactly the situation for which full employment had been devised—providing employment security only for boom times doesn't mean much. But to the extent that IBM grew bureaucratic and arrogant in its dealings with customers, thus undercutting its market, rank-and-file IBMers must accept some responsibility for the firm's reversals.

Since much of the blame for IBM's difficulties in the 1990s did not rest with employees, when the company began to lay people off, it was not responding to the employees' failure to keep up their side of the social contract, but abrogating a social contract to which employees were still largely faithful.

Although the company has not released the data, unofficial indications are that IBM's attitude surveys now show much greater distrust of management than in the past. In our opinion, this distrust is merited. The company's executive team demonstrated that it could not manage the company profitably in the difficult setting of the early 1990s, and despite new faces at the top, most of the old management group is still in place. And IBM's executives, in abandoning full employment, laid the burden of management's failures on the shoulders of employees. Promises have been broken, creating a problem for IBM in the mid-1990s.

# PART THREE

# A COMPANY IN CRISIS

# Hitting the Wall

THE STORY of IBM's poor financial performance in the early 1990s has been so extensively told elsewhere that only a few points need be made here. The firm's revenues peaked in 1990 at $68.2 billion and then edged steadily downward to $62.7 billion in 1993. Consolidated profits peaked at $5.9 billion in 1990 and then turned into losses—a net loss applicable to shareholders of $5.01 per share in 1991, $8.70 in 1992, and a whopping $14.22 in 1993.[1]

So large were the losses that some financial analysts have argued that IBM has no right to exist as a business—because it has created no value for its shareholders since the 1960s. This argument is based on comparisons of IBM's total return to its shareholders, including the partial recovery of share price in 1995, with what an investor might have earned simply by investing in an index fund (that is, a mutual fund that owns shares in a representative sample of the companies listed on the stock exchanges). IBM's leadership added nothing, this analysis suggests, to shareholder's advantage during all these years. (See Figure 9.3 in Chapter 9, showing first stagnation and then a steady deterioration after the early 1970s in IBM's share price relative to that of the Standard and Poor's 500.)

IBM's reversal of fortune is all the more pronounced because for many decades the firm had experienced an almost clockwork-like growth in revenues and profits. (See Figure 2.1, in Chapter 2.) This steady-growth pattern had defied both the nature of the information-technology industry and swings in the business cycle.

## WHAT THE NUMBERS TELL US

### What Losses?

It is difficult to get the complete story about IBM's financial performance from press accounts; for this, one must turn directly to the firm's annual reports with a sharp pencil and paper in hand. It will probably surprise most readers to learn that despite the gripping accounts of multi-billion-dollar losses rocking its stock price, IBM *has yet to report an annual operating loss in its accounts.*

In fact, IBM had operating earnings of almost $3 billion in 1991, more than $3 billion in 1992, and about $300 million in 1993, the first two quarters of which were especially turbulent due to the highly publicized turnover in CEOs. The so-called losses that triggered so much attention in the press and on Wall Street were largely due to restructuring charges—more than $24 billion taken between 1991 and 1993, inclusive. But why should anyone care if the accountants report losses in terms of restructuring charges rather than operating losses? Isn't a loss a loss?

Firms recognize the obsolescence of products, plants, or people through restructuring charges. When money is to be spent dismissing people or closing facilities over several years, prudent practice dictates that a firm capitalize the expense (that is, recognize it all at once and not spread it out as spent), so that later results reflect ongoing activity, not costs associated with past decisions. How such a charge-off is actually recorded is entirely in management's discretion. The reader may pause to consider the implications; IBM voluntarily put itself deep in the red.[2] Why would IBM do this when there are other ways to cut costs and redirect activities that have no such consequences?

IBM managers have always prided themselves on their fiscal conservatism, and taking large reserves for restructuring is the conservative approach to the problem. Beyond this, it is difficult to see any reason for resorting to restructuring charges and thus crushing IBM's reported income.

Asked about the restructuring charges, a top executive of IBM at the time indicated that the company did not have to take the huge restructuring charges. "Did the accountants insist?" we asked. "No," he replied. "But semiconductor plants for chips for mainframes were expensive to build when we needed them and expensive to write off when we didn't." He paused, then added, "The write-offs were part of turning the big ship around." Unfortunately, it appears that IBM has managed its restructuring in a way that maximized the damage done to the firm's standing and its possibilities for subsequent recovery.

John Akers certainly never foresaw year after year of restructuring charges undertaken to preserve practices like full employment. Undoubtedly, he thought that IBM's profitability was in short-term decline, a situation that required him to take short-term actions to shore up the business. He sought to sustain IBM's existing culture rather than to reshape or even possibly destroy it for short-term gains.

In all probability, Akers expected that the restructuring charges of less than $4 billion in 1991 would complete the process. Then came $11 billion in 1992, and $9 billion more in 1993. What began as a prudent fiscal practice became a burden under which IBM's finances and Akers's own career collapsed. And in an ironic twist, the financial charges that Akers took positioned his successor to lead a financial turnaround of the company.

Those who defend IBM's action point to the sharp decline in mainframe revenues during the early 1990s. This business was collapsing, and IBM's mainframe division had many redundant plants to close; the proper way to account for the costs of such actions was to recognize the losses all at once.

Usually firms do not face a sudden collapse of major markets; aging products have a slow decline, which limits restructuring charges. Information-technology markets seem to be an exception to this rule of orderly decline in product revenues; transition in this industry can be so rapid that there is no choice but to shut facilities and release people quickly—triggering huge restructuring charges. IBM is not alone in this; Digital Equipment Corporation, Data General, and Wang, to name a few others, have been similarly hit. But an experienced firm like IBM should have known that key products can collapse and that it would need to remain flexible and responsive.

It is true, of course, that had IBM not reduced its employment levels and closed facilities, with their consequent restructuring charges, the company would most likely have suffered large operating losses as costs exceeded revenues. But in managing the decline of the mainframe, IBM showed itself to be inflexible until it was too late to do anything but undertake major restructuring.

IBM's early choices clearly ignored the many other alternatives available. The firm could have tried to implement more salary and benefit cost reductions and more involuntary discharges for poor performance, and it could have offered less lucrative early retirement programs once it became clear that its costs were falling out of line with revenues. But it did not.

### Understanding the Nature of IBM's fiscal Problems

IBM's real fiscal problems are not found on its balance sheet among the restructuring charges but are buried in its income statement. The firm faced a steady long-run decline in operating margins that until very recently has shown little sign of turning around.[3] Since as least the mid-1950s, IBM's revenues have been dependent on the sale and service of large proprietary computers and related supplies that could be relied on to generate operating margins in excess of 55 percent; for every dollar's worth of product IBM sold, it could add 55 cents to its operating income.

With the ongoing slump in demand for mainframes, IBM has been forced to cut the effective price per unit of computing power offered across its mainframe product base much faster than in the past and far faster than internal improvements could cut the costs of building and selling these machines. The net result has been an erosion in operating margins to just below 40 percent by 1993, and operating margins below 40 percent are not rich enough to support IBM's existing overhead expenses.

In 1990, for example, IBM's sales, general, and administrative (SG&A) expenses—the cost of selling products and services and of administering the company—were 30 percent of income. By 1993, that percentage had declined by only one point, to 29 percent, even with all of the firm's restructuring. (This is a good indication that "restructuring" was viewed as a short-term correction and not a change in underlying practices.)

As long as gross margins were high, profitability remained good; even with high SG&A expenses. In 1990, for example, when margins were around 55 percent and SG&A was about 30 percent, IBM made

16 percent profit after all other expenses and reported record net earnings. As margins continued to fall and recorded expenses did not, however, profitability vanished; in 1993, with margins at 39 percent and SG&A at 29 percent only 1 percent remained as profit after other expenses (and before restructuring charges).

What is especially disturbing is that under Akers, IBM was unable to cut SG&A more quickly and effectively. This cost category provides the best measure of excess staffing, poor procedures, and other aspects of bureaucracy, and this number was high. Comparisons with other firms suggest that SG&A at IBM should have been cut by a third—something that chief executive Lou Gerstner came close to accomplishing after only two years on the job.

IBM thus faces a difficult period financially: It must find a replacement for the old-line mainframe with high margins even as it cuts expenses. How did IBM get in this fix?

## AN ERROR OF SUCH MAGNITUDE . . .

Early in 1980, IBM reviewed the trends of the day and made what turned out to be one of the largest miscalculations in business history. The firm concluded that it should continue building itself up to support $100 billion in sales by fiscal 1990. This target represented a doubling of then-current revenues but was seen as an "aggressive but achievable" ten-year target for a business then enjoying a recovery from the 1979 oil-shock recession in mainframe sales, the restoration of margins that had collapsed in the wake of the 4300 pricing fiasco, and the end of computer leasing, which promised to force customers to buy machines outright.

Arrogance was growing. IBM executives became very excited about seeing the company grow to $100 billion in annual revenues by 1990. At the Ryetown, New York, Hilton Conference Center, John Opel hosted a dinner after a board of directors meeting. In his remarks, the chairman noted that in the previous year IBM's rise in revenues was as big as Digital's total revenues, which was in itself as large as the revenues of all other major competitors combined. Every year, he told his audience, IBM would grow by an amount that would equal the size of Digital. IBM's only real threat, Opel said, came from Japanese competitors who with the help of their government would copy IBM's products. To beat them, IBM had to be the low-cost producer. This meant that the company had to have large new capacity for mainframe computers.

John Opel's position was that if IBM had the best products and manufacturing, then it would win in the marketplace. He saw the huge barriers to entry into semiconductor manufacturing—hundreds of millions of dollars for plant and equipment—as a big advantage to IBM, with its size and financial strength. The name of the game was low-cost manufacturing, and IBM could play through capital investment. Sales and marketing now began to be seen as a necessary evil. IBM, which had been a marketing company, now began its unhappy transition toward something else.

In 1980 IBM published its first ever corporate strategy, which articulated several key goals, none of which was customer-focused: to grow the business; to be the most profitable firm in the industry; and to compete where IBM—and not its customers—chose. Symptomatic of the growing hubris of the company, the corporate strategy insisted that IBM would do business on its own terms, not those of the customer or the marketplace.

To fund the new capacity, IBM had to have more investment dollars. To get them, IBM accelerated its movement from renting to sales. Specifically, IBM pushed sales financed by leases provided to its customers by IBM itself or by financial institutions. Prior to the end of the 1980s, American firms did not have to consolidate their leasing/ finance subsidiaries (even if wholly owned), so corporations could book leased equipment as sales. Thus, in order to raise cash for investment, the shift from rentals to leases was shown by the company as an increase in sales. This decision was to have an enormous adverse impact on IBM's customer relations.

IBM managers responded to the forecast and related growth plan by hiring tens of thousands of employees and adding billions of dollars in plant and equipment to IBM's balance sheet. In retrospect they were wildly optimistic; even negligently so.

Building and equipment contractors recall IBM's lavish spending during the years of the great capacity build-up. In Fishkill, New York, for example, IBM built semiconductor plants with the requisite super-clean rooms; the plants were built at double speed—at enormous cost— and two years after they were opened, they were shut down. In California, too, facilities were built at breakneck speed. Laboratories were opened and then shut down, dismantled, and rebuilt: In the name of speed, mistakes costing tens of millions of dollars had been made.

To finance such extravagance IBM accelerated its transition from a revenue stream of 85 percent rentals (it had been 95 percent in the distant past) to only 12 percent. IBM was abandoning its great foundation of guaranteed revenue—the rental base.

In 1985, a peak year for IBM's revenue and profits, few recognized that the company's strong performance was largely a bubble from the sell-off of rental equipment. With its rental revenue stream reduced to only about 12 percent of the total, to which was added another 30 percent of revenue from contract maintenance, only 42 percent of IBM's revenue did not need to be recreated each year. By the early 1990s, rentals were only about 4 percent and maintenance about 29 percent of revenue. IBM had converted its stable revenue stream to one that fluctuated with the economy and with the intensity of competition in its industry.

With the reduction of its rental base, IBM lost both customer loyalty and revenue stability. IBM's leadership was liquidating the company without realizing it.

Both the revenue forecast of 1980 and the growth plan derived from it were seriously flawed. They went badly awry in forecasting mainframes rather than networked microcomputers as the driving force in the future of information technology. Instead of a steady, rapid rise in mainframe sales, this sector stagnated; industry growth came from microcomputer hardware, software, and service sales.

By 1990 IBM's annual sales were about $68 billion, not $100 billion, and the firm was struggling with resource imbalances among its business segments. The strategic plan of 1980 led IBM up a hill of additional capacity and down it again. First IBM spent money to build the capacity and add people; then IBM spent money to dismantle capacity and shed people. This dynamic was the source of the huge financial write-offs that crushed the firm's profitability in the early 1990s.

Under the terms of IBM's full employment practice, literally tens of thousands of staff hired into IBM's mainframe operations had to be kept on or bought out with costly severance packages. To keep people gainfully occupied and avoid layoffs or retraining and relocation costs, some managers may have continued unnecessary work, thus delaying corrective actions. At the same time, the firm's infrastructure could not support the surging microcomputer sector because assets were tied up in mainframes.

A major forecasting error can seriously cripple a company—especially one that attempts to provide lifetime employment. As Professor Evsey Domar has said of Russia today, it is very difficult to change an economy under the condition that everyone is employed all the time. For this reason, growth planning is normally done on a very conservative and deliberate basis, in a climate of caution that in 1980 IBM failed to achieve.

As IBM built capacity, it promised investors great returns; instead they got losses and a collapsing share price. No wonder that by the early 1990s investor analysts believed that the company's executives had lied to them. Consequently, Wall Street ceased to listen to the company's management, and IBM's executives entered a black hole— nothing they could say favorably affected the company's fortunes.

## MALADMINISTRATION OF IBM's SOCIAL CONTRACT

As if all this were not enough bad news, IBM's arrogance in the early 1980s led it to undermine its social contract with its employees. During the company's boom, its managers began to treat its no-layoff practice as a "no-performance policy," that is, even poorly performing employees became immune from losing their jobs.

There was little justification for this lapse. Already there were disturbing indications that IBM's social contract was no longer serving the company well, and that it ought to be tightened, not loosened. Yet IBM let itself be blinded by the appearance of financial success into sharing an unrealistic largess with its employees.

IBM's most important warning of the need for changes in its social contract had come in the late 1960s, when IBM was reaping substantial financial rewards from its innovative System/360. But the 360 was a modular design, which allowed other vendors to build elements that would fit into IBM's basic architecture. In 1967, twelve engineers from IBM's San Jose facility quit to form their own company supplying disk drives. For this fundamental violation of IBM's loyalty contract with key employees, the twelve became known at IBM as the "dirty dozen."

But they were successful, and soon their opportunism was mimicked by others. In the late 1960s, IBM still had more than 97 percent of the disk drive market. But as IBMers left IBM to create competing firms, IBM's grip on disk drives weakened greatly.[4]

The loyalty contract began to look like a one-way bargain. But IBM made no major changes in the contract except to strengthen it. In the late 1960s, all IBMers were placed on salary, and the full-employment practice was made more explicit. Disregarding the emergence of competitors, often created by former IBMers, in the 1980s IBM further loosened the employee side of the social contract.

IBM's full employment practice was often misstated to imply that its employees enjoyed a lifetime employment guarantee. In reality, the company promised that if an employee's job were eliminated, for whatever reason, it would find the employee another assignment— provided he or she had performed satisfactorily in the past job. Control over IBM's performance appraisal system had always remained with management, allowing the firm to define satisfactory performance as needed to meet business requirements.

Unfortunately, in IBM's rapid expansion through the 1970s and 1980s, a number of relatively poor performers were added to the payroll and could not be promptly weeded out due to an inappropriately targeted performance appraisal system. In part, this targeting failure was due to choices made when the performance appraisal system was initially designed, rather than to a misapplication of the system by management. The performance and planning process was intended to help employees address job performance issues in the context of a firm that had IBM's principle of respect for the individual as one of its cultural cornerstones. As constructed, the performance system measured individuals against objective and specific criteria that they themselves helped to set in management-by-objectives sessions held with their managers. Appraisal data thus consisted of a stream of individual performance ratings; it could not be used to compare employees—a process of performance ranking—unless management deliberately violated the notion of respect for the individual and arbitrarily created common performance objectives out of the individually set objectives.

If IBM management had used straight appraisal data to make ranking decisions and had then proceeded to dismiss significant numbers of employees based on the results, the employees could have appealed their terminations on the grounds that these actions had been taken arbitrarily, and they would have been completely correct. Local IBM management, unwilling to take on the headache of designing a supplement for the appraisal system that would support effective employee ranking and could stand up against charges of arbitrary action, found an easier path, but one that hurt the firm in the long-run: They dumped their problem employees on others through internal transfers.

It is at this point that top management can be said to have failed: They did not understand until much too late in the day that their performance appraisal system was not up to the task of ranking employees and that their managers were unwilling to cull out poor performers. It was not until billions of dollars had been spent on early retirement and voluntary severance that changes were made to the appraisal system to include ranking so that marginal contributors could be identified and removed for cause.

Other firms have tackled the sensitive issue of relative performance more openly. Microsoft, for example, is said to ask members of each of its development groups to rate each other every six months and then to dismiss those in the lowest 5 percent of the averaged ratings.[5] We do not suggest that IBM should have adopted a Microsoft-style appraisal policy because peer review may discourage teamwork; but a version of the Microsoft approach would have done much to keep IBM in fighting trim. Instead, IBM went too far the other way.

During the 1980s, involuntary turnover at IBM fell to about 1 percent per annum. In effect, the full employment practice began to mean that once hired, an employee had employment security so long as his or her performance was not totally unacceptable. This erosion of standards was costly. In a survey of employee attitudes at IBM one of us conducted in 1985, the most common complaint registered was that managers were too tolerant of poor performers. In Table 6.1, we show that if IBM had rejected poor performers at two-fifths the rate attributed to Microsoft[6] and had enforced a hiring freeze, it could have achieved a headcount reduction of more than 120,000 from 1989 to 1993, without expensive early retirement and voluntary severance plans—substantially reducing its need for layoffs.

In 1990, the head of the field sales force sought authority to step up involuntary separations to 15 percent of the sales force. At the time the rate was between 1 and 2 percent. A confrontation over the matter

*Table 6.1*  Managing Employee Headcount

| Year end | Reported regular full-time employees | Projected number of full-time employees (after taking turnover, retirement, and dismissal into consideration) | Number of turnovers expected | Number of retirements expected | Number of employees who should be dismissed for poor performance | Total number of voluntary and involuntary turnovers expected |
|---|---|---|---|---|---|---|
| 1988 | 387,112 | 387,112 | | | | |
| 1989 | 383,220 | 359,379 | 10,065 | 9,926 | 7,742 | 27,733 |
| 1990 | 373,289 | 333,633 | 9,344 | 9,215 | 7,188 | 25,746 |
| 1991 | 344,396 | 309,731 | 8,674 | 8,555 | 6,673 | 23,902 |
| 1992 | 301,542 | 287,541 | 8,053 | 7,942 | 6,195 | 22,189 |
| 3Q 1993 | 267,000 | 266,942 | 7,476 | 7,373 | 5,751 | 20,600 |
| Total | | | 43,612 | 43,010 | 33,548 | 120,170 |

Assumptions:

Turnover rate: 2.60% (assuming turnover rate of engineers is applicable to the whole company)

Retirement rate: 2.56% (assuming employees are evenly distributed between ages 22 and 60)

Dismissal rate: 2.00% (assuming this is the percentage of poor performers at IBM who should be dismissed)

The company is projected to have 255,000 employees by year-end 1993 (1993 Third Quarter Report).

occurred in the management committee. Refused permission, the field sales force resorted to expensive buyouts and reduced its numbers by some 15,000 people in the next fifteen months.

IBM executives have defended the company's involuntary separation record. IBM's discharge rate was not unreasonably low, they argue, when compared to those of other large companies. IBM's discharge rate was as great as or greater than those of firms like AT&T, GTE, and several large financial institutions. Given the generally high caliber of IBM's employees and the company ethic of hard work, IBM executives thought the firm ought to have limited involuntary turnover; they were pleased when discharge rates at IBM seldom exceeded those at the large firms with which it compared itself. But were these the firms to which IBM should have been comparing itself?

The products demanded by IBM's marketplace commanded much narrower profit margins than products provided by AT&T or GTE. Using these old monopolies as benchmarks deluded IBM management into overlooking conditions at its smaller and nimbler competitors. When IBM suddenly had too many employees and needed a different style of employee performance than in the past, it should have adjusted performance criteria and lifted its involuntary discharge rate far above that of the old-line firms with which it ordinarily compared itself. Because it did not, IBM assumed an enormous financial burden when finally forced to downsize.

Did IBM's full employment practice cause the company's difficulties? No. There is little evidence that the policy made most people lazy or inept; instead it provided security to those who do their best work in a secure situation. But some employees undoubtedly took advantage of the practice to do little, and IBM's managers were lax in ferreting them out. Full employment may not have crippled IBM, but its maladministration helped to do so.

It is worth noting, again, that had IBM managed its social contract as forcefully in the 1980s as it had done in the 1960s, it could have avoided many of the restructuring charges that it was later forced to take with such damaging consequences for its financial performance.

## BUREAUCRACY AT IBM

As indicated in Chapter 3, IBM chief executives had long been concerned about bureaucratic inertia in the company. "Bureaucracy is not something that grows only in government bureaus," Thomas J. Watson, Jr., wrote in a memo to IBM managers in the mid-1960s. "It can grow in any organization, large or small, if we lose sight of the fact that individual success and corporate success are inseparable."[7]

Watson was implying that when managers care more about their careers—climbing the corporate ladder by attaining higher positions and building administrative empires—than about their company's overall business purpose, bureaucracy has a foothold and might ultimately undermine the firm.

What does *bureaucracy* mean in a business context? Watson didn't spell it out, but other successful business executives have. Tom Melohn, for example, purchased a failing firm and turned it around. Among the five key elements he cites for keeping a company successful is "Never, ever let bureaucracy sneak in."[8] Melohn defines bureaucracy as too many layers of management and too many staff and assistant positions (including clerical jobs). Melohn seems concerned with particular jobs and with a firm's overall structure. He believes small firms are more effective than large ones because small firms can more easily avoid bureaucracy. Perhaps he is right, but IBM's chief executives have nonetheless fought vigorous battles against bureaucracy.

In recent years, however, they have been losing the battle. This may be because IBM has violated the strictures against bureaucracy that Melohn and many others have found necessary to combat it.

First, IBM has many layers of management. At one count in the late 1980s there were seventeen layers of management from the chief executive to the supervisor on a factory floor or in a sales branch. Other large companies got themselves into similar situations and have been trying to work their way out. When Jack Welch took over GE in 1980, he found seventeen layers of management; today there are seven. Perhaps seven isn't the right number—perhaps six or eight might be better—but seventeen layers were certainly too many. Companies not much smaller than IBM—for example, Federal Express—have operated with only four layers and have kept stubbornly to that number despite considerable growth over many years. IBM let its management layers increase and has been slow to reduce them.

Why do too many management layers contribute to bureaucracy? Because they remove decision-making from the people who are close to the customer or to production and who are thus better able to act quickly and efficiently in the firm's interests. In addition, they promote a subculture of status-seeking, politicking for position and resources, and empire-building, each of which saps the energy of the organization and diverts it from making the business a success. Melohn puts it succinctly: successful businesses don't need many layers of management because "each of us is a boss."[9]

Second, IBM's use of staff has been excessive. In fact, the contention system by which IBM was managed for years (described in Chapter 8) required large staffs and gave them powers and responsibilities unequaled elsewhere in the industry. Melohn writes that the argument that staff free a manager to do more important things is wrong. If the tasks to be handled by staff are important, the manager should do them; if not, they needn't be done at all. Basically, Melohn argues, work assigned to staff people is generally of low priority and can largely be dispensed with. If he exaggerates, it is a pardonable exaggeration to make an important point.

Certainly staff functions are necessary in some areas. For example, the complexity of compensation systems and employment law make a personnel office necessary; the litigious American legal environment makes a corporate counsel's office necessary; some internal auditors are required in all but the smallest firms; and the sophistication of financial instruments today requires an internal finance function. Melohn knows that some limited staff functions are necessary, but he also knows that companies (including IBM) often go far beyond this necessary minimum, establishing staff functions with large numbers of employees and giving executives staff managers to help run the business.

Third, IBM has made extensive use of assistant positions. These assignments, seen as major steps in grooming a young person for later managerial and executive positions, were highly coveted in IBM, and few executives failed to have a covey of assistants and former assistants. But Melohn dismisses the rationale for assistants: An aspiring executive, he asserts, learns better by doing than by watching. Up-and-coming executives should be given line positions so they can learn from making decisions and taking actions, not staff positions in which they must remain passive.

To IBM's credit, it tried to enhance the assignments of the many assistants by allowing them, when the executives were absent, to perform the executive's job—taking inquiries and handling matters. But this experience rarely extended to significant decisions.

In summary, IBM continually made extensive use of multiple layers of management, large staffs, and assistant positions—which critics find at the heart of bureaucracy—while its chief executives railed against bureaucracy. No wonder they made so little headway. IBM chief executives rightly campaigned against the symptoms of bureaucracy—rigidity in decision making, reluctance to take action, and lack of imagination in running the business—but in recent years they failed to connect IBM's structure and management with the behavior of its employees. They seemed to believe that if IBMers would only do so, they could behave in efficient and innovative ways, despite the web of checks, balances, oversight, and red tape in which they were meshed. This was naive in the extreme.

Observers may be justified in demanding that IBM curb its bureaucratic structures and behavior; but they may err in concluding that IBM's decades of generous margins have led it to employ too many people who justify their pay by enforcing procedures rather than satisfying customers. Bureaucracy is not a simple matter of too many people, to be solved by undertaking a detailed review to find and dismiss excess staff. It is more a matter of attitude, behavior, and processes.

The rise of bureaucracy at IBM is characterized by the unwillingness of people to risk their jobs by changing the habits that had led to the firm's success, even when those habits became dated. This unwillingness to change—not excess people—has periodically led to IBM's ineffectiveness in the marketplace. Overstaffing is a symptom, not the cause, of IBM's trouble, and while layoffs may produce short-term financial gain, if handled improperly they will dilute IBM's social contract. This outcome, as we have already seen, is likely to hurt the firm in the long run.

Throughout IBM's history, managers have "bet the company," spending billions with entrepreneurial zeal on new technology and creating thousands of new jobs. In part they were able to do this because they were not busy downsizing to get rid of people deemed surplus following a past product transition. And, as we have shown before, the 1980s were not the first time IBM had suffered from bureaucratic rigidity; in fact, bureaucracy characterized by rigidity of attitude has always lurked at IBM.

## ECONOMIC CIRCUMSTANCES

Despite being sensitive to economic conditions in its major markets, from the 1930s through much of the 1980s IBM was nearly always able to generate increasing profits because of its international diversification. Through the IBM World Trade Corporation and national subsidiaries in Europe and Japan, the parent firm could rely on non–U.S. economic growth when the United States was in recession, and vice versa. Few were the times when all areas of the developed world went into boom or recession simultaneously.

As the world economy has developed floating exchange rates, round-the-clock currency trading, and much broader flows of trade and credit among key nations, the degree of diversification in underlying economic conditions around the globe has diminished. The leaders of the G7 nations, the United States, the European Union, Japan, and others, have all recognized that they can no longer pursue divergent fiscal or monetary policies without domestic consequences such as falling terms of trade, rising prices, or job loss.

On the one hand, this is a positive development: It greatly reduces the prospect of global conflict, because it is bad business to shoot at one's customers. On the other hand, for firms such as IBM, it is a negative development, since it substitutes a *global* business cycle for the multiple *national* cycles of the past, making it very difficult for large-scale capital-goods producers to avoid the customary fallout of a cyclical downturn.

In the early 1990s, for the first time in many years, all of IBM's major markets went into prolonged recession simultaneously. With all markets in recession, IBM's prospects were further diminished by its excess production capacity as well as by that of other mainframe makers, who were in even worse straits because of their smaller market shares and who were therefore even more desperate to cover the variable costs of production by selling mainframes at sharp discounts.

Some of IBM's difficulties in the 1990s can thus be blamed on the world economy rather than on management, as shown in our regression analysis of IBM's inflation-adjusted after-tax income against the gross domestic products, at constant price level, of IBM's three principal markets, the United States, Europe, and Japan. (See Appendix.) We found that almost half of the variations in IBM's income coincided with variations in the GDP of those markets.

# Paradigm Paralysis

"**I**BM DEVELOPED paradigm paralysis," a customer told us during an interview. "They got stuck in a mode of believing that things were going to stay as they were forever. They missed the boat, believing that the mainframe would be around forever. They were behind the curve when the world changed."

## MARKETING WAS KING

Throughout IBM's long history marketing has been king in the firm. Because its connections to the major buyers of information technology have been so much closer than those of its rivals, IBM has been called a marketer with a strong technology-development arm. IBM's closeness to its customers explains how the firm could so often be late with new technology—or could even for long periods offer products less effective than those of its competitors—and yet come back to dominate the industry. It wasn't enough for IBM's competitors to develop superior technology; to displace IBM, they also needed effective marketing strategies and sales forces capable of executing these strategies—a package few of them have ever managed to put together.

IBM's marketing orientation permeated it from top to bottom. It used to surprise students of management that IBM chief executives so often had liberal arts and business educations and marketing backgrounds rather than engineering degrees and production backgrounds.

But the company was co-founded by a salesman who learned his trade in the field, and most of his successors have followed him out of marketing.

Years ago, one of us asked an IBM executive to name the major contribution that Tom Watson, Sr., had made to the firm. The expected answer was a statement citing IBM's three basic values—respect for the individual, pursuit of excellence, and the best customer service—or praising his building of a great sales organization. Instead the executive thought for several moments, then responded, "He chose the business that we're in." That is a remarkable answer for several reasons.

First, it was the opposite of a technologist's answer. The implication was that the group of people who were IBM at that time—executives, managers, professionals, salespersons, clerical workers, and factory workers—could have been in some other business. No person who loved the technology could have given such a response. Such an answer would never be offered by managers of most computer firms, which are made up of people who love the technology and find themselves working together because of this shared love.

Second, the answer was remarkable because it reflected exactly what a chief executive should do—make strategic decisions about such crucial questions as "What business should we be in?" Thinking about technology needed to make the business go is the province of engineers. Technology is the means, not the end, for a marketing company.

But more than a chief executive's marketing background was required to turn an IBM into a marketing powerhouse; also contributing was the firm's megastrategy based on singleness and employee loyalty aimed at excellence in customer service. IBM is not a natural monopoly like the postal system or the telephone company. It just seemed that way because IBM was always able to talk to the data-processing managers of very large firms and deliver the goods—as the old slogan went: "No one ever got fired for choosing IBM!"

Singleness enabled IBM to deliver the most complicated information-technology products, systems, and services within the context of one unified sales pitch and price catalog; component compatibility was almost always entirely assured before the pieces were assembled on the user site. And when the system reached the user, technicians and other support personnel worked from the same blueprints and for the same managers as did the sales representatives—if a problem arose, one telephone call summoned an army that worked until a solution was found. To a great many management-information-systems managers, IBM looked, acted, and sounded exactly like their own centrally coordinated firms.

Employee loyalty was so strong a tradition at IBM that many executives were delighted when an IBM manager left the company for a position with a customer. IBM alumni could not give away leading-edge technology to a rival or a customer; instead the alumni tightened links to IBM. Who else knew better where to get service for an IBM installation than the ex-IBMer who was helping to run it?

## WHAT WENT WRONG?

It is tempting to blame IBM's leadership for most or all of its troubles, and in Chapter 8 we will look more closely at this aspect of IBM's story. Only by looking beyond executive decision-making to the systems that failed and the circumstances under which they failed, however, can an analysis such as this hope to inform readers about what to avoid in their own organizations. Two general points will help to set the context for understanding the root causes of IBM's troubles. First, IBM's rank-and-file were not to blame. Furthermore, blame placed on the firm's culture is appropriate only to the extent that IBM's approximately one thousand top managers worldwide failed to use properly the established management systems. Despite all that has been written about the white shirts and blue suits, the company's refusal to serve alcohol at its functions, and other aspects of the firm's culture, these things are simply irrelevant. Second, some of the causes were external to the firm; that is, given similar economic and other circumstances to those that prevailed at IBM, any firm might have slipped. Monday-morning quarterbacking is easy in an industry in which market trends change quickly; the executives held responsible receive the blame, even if the problems are much more systemic.[1]

As we have seen in previous chapters, IBM's technology and product lines in the late 1980s and early 1990s were strong. But IBM was pushing products on its customers that, often, they did not want, making customer relations an important area for the investigation into IBM's difficulties.

At IBM, customer and employee relations were intertwined. Long-term employees gave customers confidence in dealing with IBM. IBM employees, for the most part, stayed with the firm out of loyalty, due largely to the firm's full employment practices, unusual in a volatile industry, and its long tradition of value-driven leadership.

Despite these strengths, IBM in the mid-1980s disrupted first its relationships with its customers and later its relationships with its employees because of its build-up of excess capacity. Poor employee relations only worsened already weakened customer relations as dissatisfied employees became unsatisfactory customer representatives.

During the 1980s build-up, IBM's new factories, operating at full capacity, spewed out vast quantities of product in order to get the lowest cost per unit and therefore provide the best possible price to customers. Sales representatives had to push the iron in order to keep the factories operating. Each customer, however, had its own priorities.

John Akers's reality became no one else's—certainly not that of his customers. IBM hoped to sell products to customers because it was the low-cost producer; customers would take what IBM produced because IBM, not they, knew what they needed.

IBM thought it could manage its customers' expectations; that customers expected too much of the company and could be brought to expect less. But IBM couldn't do this; its customers had alternatives to buying from IBM.

At this time, IBM's client representatives were supposed to sell IBM; customer relations were of little concern. When customers began to ask for items other than what IBM produced and the field sales organization asked for permission to sell solutions that included hardware and software from other firms, the answer from the top was no. Those in the field were to do only one thing—sell IBM's capacity.

An IBM salesperson said of this period, "When a customer would say he or she wanted something we didn't have on the shelf, we'd respond, 'You don't really need that. If you did, we'd have it. We're the experts. Let us show you what you really need from our list of products.' " So much for the customer being king, or a firm being customer-driven. A better depiction would be IBM as customer-driving. It's no surprise that major customers soon became fed up with this approach.

But the story is even worse. IBM had traditionally rented its equipment. In the 1950s, more than 90 percent of the firm's receipts were from rentals. A salesperson's responsibility was first to maintain the stream of receipts from existing rentals and only then to add to it. But in the 1970s and 1980s, IBM shifted from rentals to sales. Initially this was a response to a large amount of dated inventory in an IBM division that wanted to get rid of it fast by low-priced sales. Fortuitously, it then appeared, sales swelled revenues much more quickly than had rentals, and soon the entire company was hooked on selling. The enhanced cash flow helped the company pay for its expansion in the 1980s. By 1990, the company drew 85 percent of its revenues from sales. Rentals were a fading memory.

When renting gave way to selling, the rhythm of IBM's business changed from relationship-selling to transaction-selling. In the old approach, IBM sold systems—for example, a payroll system—rather than the hardware on which it ran. In consequence, the old IBM was a partner to its customer, with IBM owning the hardware that the customer used and being responsible day by day for the successful operation of the payroll system. IBM had its assets at stake just as its customers did. In this mode, IBM sold to its customers' operating managers (or their information-system directors) and retained a strong communication link with them.

Under the new system, the measure of relative progress or lack of it with each customer was gone. If IBM lost one customer, it searched for another. The field sales force pushed the iron, selling the capacity of IBM's plants by discounts and other means, but they were no longer building relationships with customers. When IBM sold a computer to an airline, no one knew if the base with that customer was growing or not. No one was watching. To clear out plant capacity, IBM pushed product on its customers—not solutions or applications.

Unfortunately, IBM had broken off its conversation with its customers—its source of important insights into changing perceptions about quality and value—just at the time its customers were switching toward networked microcomputers and client-server technology. IBM was blind in a shifting marketplace. While IBM pressed ahead with its flawed strategy, thousands of small competitors nibbled at the giant's market share.

At the outset of the 1980s, when IBM decided to aim for $100 billion in sales in 1990, it began to add people rapidly. IBM built from the top down—that is, it promoted people, creating lower-level vacancies that were filled by hiring. It made sales representatives into managers, sucking the reps out of customers' offices and replacing them with new, inexperienced people, who, although carefully trained by IBM, were not as effective as their predecessors. Without a relationship with a sales representative, customers who had to buy, not rent, sent purchasing agents to negotiate deals rather than operating managers or data processing people. Purchasing agents cared little for IBM's reputation, and much about its prices, which often they found too high. IBM had abandoned its relationships with its customers and now lost its friends within its customers' shops. IBM's top executives didn't seem to care about the change in the relationship because they had shifted their strategy from favoring a long-term relationship with rental customers to the short-term relationship of a buy-sell transaction.

Value is determined by the customer, not the producer. And the customer redefines value over time. When a firm loses its connection to its customers, it loses the context of its business and cannot make correct decisions. This is what happened to IBM.

This was not the fault of IBM's field sales force. They had little to do with the disaster. It was not the result of a culture of complacency. Often sales managers were in tears—they were caught between the customer and IBM corporate-level decisions. There were too many salespeople in the field given the company's financial condition, but that wasn't their fault.

IBM had ceased to put its customers' concerns first and had instead substituted its own needs, with disastrous consequences in the years ahead. Peter Drucker has defined the purpose of business as getting a customer. Why was IBM in business—to keep customers or to treat them as transactions? IBM came up with the wrong answer to this question.

By the early 1990s, it was clear that something had gone terribly wrong at IBM. A premier marketing company had literally lost touch with its market. A huge and growing segment of information-technology customers no longer believed IBM was setting market standards; its service reputation was fading away and its sales force was deemed highly arrogant and fixated on technology. By switching to sales, IBM had lost touch with its customers' operating managers, who knew how operating needs were changing. This was catastrophic because it occurred just as operating managers were shifting from mainframes to client-server systems. It wasn't that IBM didn't have client-server technology—it did—but IBM didn't realize that its customers wanted it. IBM was no longer listening.

Put bluntly, customers in the past had bought solutions and reliability from IBM; then IBM moved them down to buying boxes. Soon many customers concluded that they could get cheaper boxes elsewhere.

Interestingly, writing for publication in 1990, before IBM's disastrous results were fully apparent, former chief executive Thomas J. Watson, Jr., commented, "I was alarmed when Frank [Cary, IBM's chief executive] and his eventual successor John Opel rapidly phased out the rental system, shifting billions of dollars worth of business to outright sales." He added that it "caused me to wish I were still running the show."[2]

Watson was right to be concerned. Renting had not been just a financial strategy, it had been the eyes of IBM's business.

## THE SYSTEM UNRAVELS

The system had begun to unravel. To keep its plants operating at full capacity, and therefore minimum cost per unit, IBM used its salespeople to push the product. Customer relationships were sacrificed. The company lost sight of changing customer needs. A shift in demand that should have been foreseen by IBM was missed, and sales of mainframes declined precipitously, to the company's astonishment.

Now reassignments of excess people to sales were not enough to keep profits flowing. Tens of thousands of employees were induced to take early retirement or severance packages, and billions of dollars were taken as special charges to reduce payroll. Losses piled up and costs of separation had to be reduced. So in 1992 IBM began to lay off people. The contract with employees was effectively broken.

To understand the significance of this, think of IBM as the place in the information-technology industry where people with an interest in computers and a high concern for economic security chose to go to work. These two human characteristics—interest in computers and concern for personal security—are not incompatible. Not everyone who is adept at computers is a cowboy, recklessly betting his or her career on the next product. Many people find strength to confront an uncertain marketplace through their own employment security. At the height of IBM's economic strength, at the end of the 1980s, IBM kept on its personnel files more than a million applications for employment. IBM had the pick of a huge crop from which to fill its ranks. But when the company ended its full employment practice, people who had chosen IBM because of the promise of security were deeply demoralized. IBM statistics from employee opinion surveys have not been made public, but dissatisfaction within the company seems to have become widespread and performance suffered.

This completed the downward spiral. A shift from renting to sales and an overbuilding of capacity led to a violation of an implicit contract with customers and then to violation of an implicit contract with employees. Employees, embittered, lost confidence in the company, and many of the best performers—who could most easily find alternative employment—left. Productivity slipped. The company downsized by half: 200,000 jobs disappeared. John Akers, the chief executive officer, lost his job, and IBM for the first time in its history was turned over to an outsider to run.

Lost in a vast amount of red ink, the old IBM with its strong culture and market dominance disappeared.

## ANGRY CUSTOMERS

Despite IBM's desertion of its close relationship with customers, many still saw IBM as a leader in information technology and were frustrated at having to shop around. They were angry that IBM no longer simplified their lives by keeping order in the information-technology marketplace, and they were bitter that buying IBM was no longer a secure, unassailable decision. IBM had let its customers down—gone was simplicity, gone was order, gone was security. A more disillusioned, frustrated, and angry group of people than IBM's former customers is hard to find. How did this happen? How did IBM drift away from its model of past success? In the spring of 1994, our researchers asked a number of former IBM customers to tell us what they thought. We conducted lengthy interviews with representatives of more than one hundred firms, half of which were Fortune 1000 firms and the other half somewhat smaller. We talked primarily to information-technology executives, and we coded the open-ended discussions using content analysis. Their responses are summarized below.

## Losing Touch with the Marketplace

The most frequent and significant complaint made by the IBM customers interviewed—37 percent—was that IBM lost touch with the marketplace. This is a surprising indictment of a company that, as we have seen, was built on decades of marketing success, of striving to stay in touch with customers.

"They got out of touch with the needs of their customers," one respondent told us. "They got too far removed from the day-to-day issues facing customers," echoed another. "IBM got into trouble because of greed and stupidity. They thought about themselves and not the customer," said a third. Similar condemnations of IBM's sales representatives were repeated to us continually, as the following sampling shows.

- "IBM made products and thought they could make people buy them instead of asking their customers what they needed and designing products to meet those needs."

- "IBM got too arrogant, rich, and narrow-minded. It failed to realize that this year's customer is different from last year's."

- "They didn't listen to the customer. They made assumptions about what the customer wanted. They listened to themselves, and their customers changed from underneath them."

On a closely related theme, many customers complained that IBM's sales force lost track of the business needs of their customers and became fixated on technology. A more ironic criticism couldn't be made. The salespeople of the industry's preeminent marketing company had become techies—and not the best techies at that. "They took a technical view of our needs," said a customer, "not a business view." Said another, "They were coming from a technology view, not a business view. They didn't understand the customer's business."

## Moving Too Slowly

Another strong theme revealed by our customer surveys—35 percent of the total—was that IBM failed to keep up with its more nimble competitors; in effect, it lost touch with the market because the market outran it. Even when the firm understood customer needs and had the technology to effect a solution, it could not make decisions when required, and was thus unable to deliver solutions on time.

In an interview, one IBM middle manager expressed the problem this way: The company did not lack business, but its competitors were getting that business. He explained.

> Often I have a request from a customer to do something special to get a sale. So I tell the customer I'll try to get right back to her or him. Then I present the customer's request to my boss, who kicks it up to his boss, and often eventually to corporate headquarters. All this takes time. Finally, I may receive a positive reply—"Go ahead and do it," I'm told, "get the business." Then I go back to my customer and I say, "We're all set. I've got approval. Let's do the deal." And my customer says to me, "You're too late. Your competitor agreed to provide what I need two weeks ago."

A survey respondent explained his dissatisfaction with IBM in related terms. "As IBM grew over the years, it got more and more specialists. All these specialists created a hierarchy in their own specialties, but few knew the entire spectrum of IBM's products. One specialist didn't know what another was doing. IBM lacked generalists."

Other customers insisted that IBM simply made a mistake of timing in delaying introduction of its own new products. "IBM milked the mainframe cash cow too long," said a customer, "and held back on technology they were developing. Any successful company has to be prepared to make obsolete its own products, and IBM wasn't prepared to do this."

## *Arrogance*

An IBM salesperson, now an executive, once explained to us how he and his associates became accustomed to dealing with customers in the late 1980s.

> When a customer would ask for something which we didn't have, I'd reply, "You don't need it. If you needed it, we'd have it on the shelf. We know your information technology needs better than you do. Let me take your problem and work out a solution using the items which we have in stock. There's no need for anything produced by any other vendor; there's no need for linking our equipment to that of any other firm; we can do

it all for you and with items off our shelf. We're the experts—let us tell you what you need."

Customers understandably saw this as arrogance on IBM's part, and 11 percent of our survey respondents cited it as major cause of IBM's decline. "They got too big for their britches," one customer told us. "When there was a problem, they wouldn't listen. Instead of fixing the problem, they would try to sell us newer, more expensive systems for which we weren't ready." "Over the years," said another customer, "their attitude turned me off, and I'm sure it must have turned others off as well. They were too arrogant and didn't want to understand our needs."

### Pricing Itself out of the Market

"We evaluated different hardware equipment vendors two years ago," reported a former customer, "including IBM. We discounted IBM immediately because their costs were so much more expensive than the others. We decided that we couldn't afford to do business with IBM." This was a distressing reversal for IBM. Years ago, firms used to decide that they couldn't afford *not* to do business with IBM, even at somewhat higher prices. When IBM set standards and provided unequaled service, customers were prepared to tolerate higher costs. But without standards or service quality, there was no reason to pay more for IBM products, and 6 percent of our survey respondents ceased doing business with IBM for this reason.

Listen to another IBM customer. "Basically, they priced themselves out of the market. In the last ten years whenever we went out for quotes and bids, IBM was always on the high end of pricing, and other reliable vendors had more cost-effective systems. IBM didn't adjust its pricing."

### Other Usual Suspects

Perhaps surprisingly, certain other usual suspects among the reasons cited by analysts for IBM's decline were not mentioned very frequently by IBM's customers in our conversations with them. IBM's desire to preserve its proprietary systems—that is, to sell a total IBM solution to a customer's data-processing problems—was cited by only 2 percent of our respondents. Similarly, the alleged internal dissension among divisions within IBM came up only rarely.

IBM customers in the mid-1990s were angry at the company for losing touch with the marketplace and with them. But we shall see in Chapter 11 that they still expect a great deal from the company.

# WHO WAS AT FAULT?

# Management's Responsibility

To WHAT degree were IBM's troubles caused by its leaders? In previous chapters we have identified some of the ingredients of IBM's difficulties—a severe economic downturn, a rising tide of bureaucracy, errors in strategic planning, and a malfunctioning social contract. These were really only symptoms of a deeper malaise, however, evidence that IBM management failed to perceive and adapt to new circumstances. But why did this broader failing occur, and who was responsible?

## WHO WAS RESPONSIBLE?

Changing course at IBM takes a long time, which makes considerations of responsibility difficult. Since 1956, IBM has had six chief executives: Thomas J. Watson, Jr., from 1956 to 1971; T. Vincent Learson, from 1971 to 1972; Frank Cary, from 1973 to 1980; John Opel, from 1981 to 1984; John Akers, from 1985 to 1992; and Louis V. Gerstner, Jr., since 1993.

It is tempting to hold each of these executives responsible for IBM's performance during his tenure, but this fails to reflect reality. Most business observers and investors today are impatient, though they often deny it. They expect things to happen quickly and look for the causes of present success or failure in the immediate past. They imagine chains of causation no longer than a year or two long.

But very large businesses occupy a different time frame; they are as they are because of decisions and events of the far—not recent—past. Managing executives often find themselves bitterly impatient at the slow pace of change and at their inability to discover the root cause within the firm's culture that is inhibiting change. Investors are even more impatient and clamor for new faces who will turn the business around quickly. But like a great tree that has taken decades to grow, a large company can be modified quickly only by hacking away with axes. It can be cut down quickly—it cannot be transformed quickly.

To take another metaphor, large firms, like large ships, cannot be turned quickly. Turns will be wide and slow, even after the captain has issued the orders. In today's impatient climate, these delays are almost intolerable to investors and pundits. Yet, in reality, change takes time.

Thus, each IBM chief executive is a captive of the decisions made by his predecessor. John Opel carried forward the expansion set in motion by Frank Cary and added to it; Akers inherited the momentum established by Opel and sought to turn the ship around, but the consequences of Cary and Opel's earlier decisions overwhelmed him. Akers set in motion a change of direction from which Gerstner has benefited. In a sense, each IBM chief executive in the past two decades has paid the price or reaped the benefits of his predecessor's decisions, while setting in motion the change of direction that would determine his successor's fate.

Investors, lacking patience for this reality, hold each chief executive accountable not for the direction in which he points the company but for what happens while he is in charge; that is, Wall Street holds the chief executive accountable for the consequences of his predecessor's choice of direction. This may be unfair, but it's no secret. IBM's chief executives act for the long term but are judged on the short term. The success or failure of a chief executive hinges on his ability to defy the tide and turn the ship quickly. At IBM, such quick course correction was made very difficult by the company's style of management.

## THE CONTENTION PROCESS

In many respects IBM is the most American of companies. Because of its many years of success, its sales representatives' famous blue-suit-

and-white-shirt uniform, and its sales meeting razzmatazz, IBM has often been considered an American icon, along with apple pie and baseball. Yet this paragon of American business style is also in many aspects one of the least representative of American companies. In particular, the way IBM has been managed is very different from management at other U.S. firms. Under contention, IBM was managed collegially. Its chairperson was first among equals, not king; decisions of the management committee were made largely by consensus. IBM was managed like a European firm, with a management board making decisions, rather than like an American firm, with a boss at the helm.

Frank Cary, John Opel, and John Akers were not alone in making the decisions that crippled IBM—they were joined by entire generation of IBM's top executives. As Paul Rizzo, IBM's vice chairman, once put it in a lecture at Harvard Business School, "Those of us on IBM's management committee have all grown up in the business and see it in much the same way. So we don't have open dissent."

Like so many of us in our own business and personal lives, IBM executives who worked closely together had fixed expectations of each other. If some of the group didn't see any need for change, the others were less likely to do so as well. Even chief executives found it difficult to make a sharp turn when those steering the ship expected to keep to a straight course.

Some analyst argue that such inertia is precisely the leadership challenge that chairpersons of large firms like IBM are called upon to meet. When other executives are unable or unwilling to initiate the difficult changes demanded by the marketplace, it is the chairperson's obligation to push change forward. This is the definition of leadership.

But this reasoning is facile. At collegially managed IBM, with its record of success, a man like John Akers—identified with the heyday of the mainframe era—naturally found it difficult to overcome his colleagues' expectations and shift dramatically the firm's course. He was too constrained by the opinions of his colleagues.

The core practices of IBM's management style have been management committees at the corporate level; a formal process of consensus building, labeled, of all things, a contention system; and a strong role for staff functions, more so than at other firms. Of these three, the most unusual—and the governing practice—was the contention system; both the use of staff and the arbitration function of the top executive committee (the Corporate Management Committee, or CMC) were expressed through the contention system.

In the late 1970s, Professor Richard Vancil of the Harvard Business School wrote a case showing IBM's contention system in action, using IBM's development of a new technology, known as the "bubble" memory, as his subject. An operating division, the General Products Division (GPD), headed by a corporate vice president, proposed a certain level of funding and scientific staffing for the project over the course of a year. The office of the chief scientist, a staff function, had reviewed the GPD plan, as it did plans from all operating divisions annually, and was disturbed by what it saw. In the opinion of the chief scientist, the bubble memory had substantial potential and might be brought to market at any time by one of IBM's competitors. The chief scientist thought the level of funding and staffing proposed for the bubble memory project was much too low and sought to change GPD's plan.

Discussions ensued between representatives of the GPD and of the office of the chief scientist. When neither side would budge, the chief scientist filed a formal statement of nonconcurrence with the CMC. Had the chief scientist not done so, his silence would have been interpreted as support for the GPD plan. The contention system did not permit a staff function to ignore or remain neutral on the plans of an operating division. The chief scientist had to review the division's plans and decide to either support or oppose them.

The contention system had great strengths and weaknesses. It ensured that the plans of each operating division were reviewed in depth and that concerns would thereby be forced into the open and addressed directly by top management. But contention was also very slow and expensive to administer: Many people spent much time carefully making and reviewing plans. Although providing a mechanism for carrying disputes right to the top, the system seemed at times to invite discord and consume top executives' time with insignificant matters.

In the bubble memory incident, GPD's plans were debated in front of the top executives on the CMC, then chaired by CEO Frank Cary, a former marketing executive with degrees in political science and management. No CMC member had a technical background, and yet the CMC was expected to resolve a dispute between the chief scientist and the head of GPD—each of whom had a Ph.D. in physics! Rarely has the character of IBM as primarily a marketing company with an interest in technology been so graphically illustrated.

After a lengthy exchange, Cary sided with the chief scientist and told GPD to triple the resources devoted to the bubble memory. The head of GPD did not agree and never did assign significant resources to the technology, a lapse that contributed to his demotion not long after. In the internal political maneuvering of IBM, the chief scientist had fired what IBMers called a silver bullet—that is, a formal nonconcurrence statement through the contention process—and had killed his opponent. But subsequent developments proved that the GPD had probably been right: The bubble memory never fulfilled its early promise. Today, the former head of GPD remains convinced that he saved IBM both financial and human resources that would have otherwise been devoted to a mediocre technology. But the then chief scientist adheres to his view that had the bubble memory been aggressively pursued, IBM would have made a major breakthrough in the technology and carried it forward successfully to market.

Why did the contention system develop? The pillar of singleness in IBM's megastrategy led the firm to view itself as one company worldwide. In practice, this meant that the management team, using an array of corporate policy directives, was continually trying to rein in the individual business units. In fact, one of the most consistent criticisms of the firm for many years was that headquarters was always imposing its views on local operations that would run more efficiently with less oversight. To balance this degree of control from the center, IBM created a mechanism to give the various units and functions a say in development of common policies. It was through the open debate of contention that strong staff groups and managers could best achieve the consensus required to help the CMC generate effective policy for the firm. It was in part to protect the diversity of opinion required to make contention work that the firm invested so heavily in its loyalty contract with employees, reinforcing cultural values—respect for the individual—with extensive benefits like full employment and the so-called voice programs, such as the Open Door, Speakout, and others. IBM needed to know that its employees and managers could disagree with one another before decisions were taken and then come together afterwards to implement them.

The bubble memory story shows IBM's contention system working as it should. The system didn't ensure that correct decisions were always reached, but it did ensure that divergent points of view were heard. Dissident opinions were voiced, and top executives made decisions that took these opinions into account, protecting the company from total disaster in the event that the dissidents turned out to be right. A system that seemed to outsiders to encourage disagreement and conflict actually promoted rough consensus in decision-making.

One of the puzzles of IBM's recent history is what caused this system to decay in the 1980s. Contention weakened in the 1970s and all but disappeared in the 1980s, as IBM top executives seemed to come to believe that the system had been most useful when the company was simpler, with fewer products and fewer people. But along with the contention system a mechanism for disagreement and debate also disappeared.

On key issues involving the personal computer, workstations, client-server systems, operating systems for personal computers, and the production of microprocessors for the general marketplace, voices of dissent in IBM were either silenced or run over roughshod. Once, discussing with a top IBM executive of the 1980s the company's failure to wrest from Microsoft the operating system for the personal computer, we suggested that this was a mistake by IBM's top executives. "Yes," he agreed, "but there were at least a thousand of us located in many different countries. Anyone could have raised an objection—and should have. But I don't remember any."

There was dissent at IBM. During John Akers's chairmanship, key issues were placed before him by members of his planning staff but failed to gain a general hearing in the management committee. Objections to the company's direction weren't made with sufficient force to affect mistaken decisions, the purpose for which the contention system had been designed. Without the contention system, key issues were not sufficiently examined and debated. Consensus, formerly developed through vigorous discussion, gave way to group-think. An essential aspect of IBM's culture was no longer functioning correctly, and the company paid a grievous price.

## MANAGEMENT BY COMMITTEE

The contention process was a formal mechanism intended to force into the open disagreements about the company's direction. Silver bullets were rare, but management committee meetings were not. The CMC, a small committee of the top executives of the firm, was often supplemented by a larger group of both line and staff executives, usually termed the Management Committee, which met monthly. At various times in the 1980s and 1990s there was one committee, or two, with changing designations; a management committee sometimes met daily—with both morning and afternoon sessions.

Were these committees effective in stimulating discussion and debate about major issues in the firm's strategy or operations? Apparently not to the extent they should have been.

Several executives who ran IBM's divisions criticized the management committees in discussions with us. The meetings were a lot of time wasted, we heard. At these meetings, the executives who ran the operating units were criticized and put on the spot to defend their positions, but not for a profit-or-loss result. In fact, incredible though it may sound, IBM had no separate profit-loss measure for some of its largest units. Executives were not being challenged for the success of failure of their businesses, but for failing to do this or that which was dear to a senior executive of the firm or to some staff executives.

This was a terrible way to run a business. It took the minds of the operating executives off the profit or loss of their businesses and focused it on other, often extraneous issues. In many instances, the issues reflected nothing but the changing complexion of corporate politics, so that executives were required to focus not on their businesses but on the politics of the top executive suite.

In this environment, presentations took on a life of their own. Management committee meetings became a theater in which operating unit executives tried to outdo one another in a contest of who had the best ideas. This was the opposite of management-by-walking-around. Instead of managers going out to visit people in the company to discover what was afoot, top managers were all brought to the mountain—to headquarters. An executive heading an IBM division would come to a management committee meeting armed with a slick presentation and assistants to present it for him. Around the edges of the room sat assistants to various executives and staff officers—a peanut gallery to whom the presenters played. So stylized did these presentations become, and of so little value in running the business, that Lou Gerstner in 1993 required executives to dispense with formal presentations by their aides and instead tell him about their businesses themselves.

Another key part of the company's culture—the tie between employment security and performance—had also ceased to function effectively at about the same time as did its contention process and management meetings. It wasn't IBM's traditional culture that led IBM into a spiral of decline, but perversions of that culture that had slipped into IBM's practices.

## WHY IBM FAVORED CONSENSUS MANAGEMENT

John Akers was chosen for the key leadership position by IBM's board of directors after a long career in IBM's mainframe marketing business; he was, in many senses, a product of the traditional path up through the ranks at IBM. He was also a consensus manager in the mold of his predecessors John Opel and Frank Cary rather than an imperial executive like Thomas J. Watson, Sr., or his son, Thomas J. Watson, Jr.

Ever since the days of Thomas J. Watson, Jr., IBM has struggled to prevent the emergence of an imperial chief executive, creating corporate management committees and the contention system to force the CEO into seeking consensus. Why did IBM do this? Why did it feel that consensus decision-making was important? The answer is that, unlike CEOs at most companies of IBM's size, IBM's leader was at the hub of a highly centralized system of authority. Even as a $60 billion company, IBM was effectively managed from the center. It was the most centralized of the world's great corporations. Wielding all of the power held by IBM's CEO could turn any manager into an autocrat. The very qualities required to become IBM's chief executive—a strong personality and self-assurance—could easily blind an individual to the merits of consulting others on decisions. One-person rule could seriously damage the firm, hence the establishment of a system of checks and balances restraining the chief executive.

Most big companies have an organizational structure studded with semi-autonomous divisions, thereby dispersing power beyond the effective reach of their chief executives. They do not need to worry about an imperial CEO because even an autocrat would have a limited reach in the top office. Not so at IBM; the highly centralized organization required by singleness concentrates power at the center, power that could easily be abused if not kept in check through contention.

Since collegiality and consensus-seeking play such an important role in IBM's management, it is wrong to blame John Opel or John Akers alone for the mistakes of IBM during their tenures. When mistakes were made, a *team* made those mistakes—not an individual. But this raises even more troubling implications. An individual, blinded by ego, might make damaging errors, but how could a group of highly experienced managers with divergent viewpoints on IBM's strategic position lose sight of the marketplace to the extent that IBM's top executives did?

Two things went wrong. First, IBM's management team became over-confident: Decades of success had led them to believe that they could continue to manage a centralized enterprise in an industry that was in reality becoming far too fragmented for exclusively top-down management; past success blinded them to their future vulnerability. Second, the contention system through which IBM had attained diversity of views contributing to critical decisions broke down. When almost all top executives brought a similar viewpoint with them to their meetings, effective debate was smothered and uniformity crippled the company.

The near uniformity in viewpoints among IBM's top managers during periods when crucial errors were made did not rule out consideration and debate of key issues. Key issues were identified by top staff and discussed with top executives; radical alternatives were proposed and rejected. The debates were substantive but the results were inadequate. The transitions faced by the information industry in the early 1980s provide an example. Three distinct approaches had surfaced: an infrastructure somewhat like an electric utility; a range of products or tools; and databases and their management. IBM had to decide on a direction for its business. It could provide infrastructure, but it had much unnecessary bureaucracy and high overhead. It could provide products, but that area was highly competitive, and IBM needed large operating profit margins to cover its high overhead; intense competition would erode IBM's margins. It could acquire and own databases, but then what would keep the huge mainframe manufacturing complex at Fishkill working?

In the end the conundrum was never resolved. IBM executives effectively acted as if these issues were too complex to be answered, the problems too big to be solved. They adopted no strategy to meet the industry's changing circumstances. Instead they chose a simpler route, treating as a strategy what was merely an extrapolation of high growth and increasing profitability.

## SUCCESS AND COMPLACENCY IN THE MID-1980s

IBM has experienced a repeating pattern in which marketplace success leads to complacency and crisis, and the 1980s provided another instance. How was it that the managers' excessive pride—not, after all, unusual in successful companies—crippled IBM? The answer lies in the peculiar features of competition in the information-technology industry.

The cycle of business in information technology starts with rounds of vicious competition, followed by virtual monopoly exploitation of technology by the winner, and culminating in copycatting of the successful products by other firms. Firms struggle to develop technology that can cut costs, improve capacity, or extend the range of tasks that computers can accomplish. Most such advances are incremental in nature; users who cannot add the advance to their existing systems do not scrap those machines for new ones offering the advance because the benefits of doing so are usually outweighed by the costs of developing new procedures, rewriting manuals, or going off-line to change systems. Only when a number of incremental advances have been made do users think about changing their basic systems.

Periodically, however, advances in technology emerge that are so sweeping that a competitor can reshape the underlying fundamentals of computing and trigger an immediate migration of users to new machines. Firms that win such competitions establish the new ground rules under which future incremental advances will occur and earn huge profits from control of these market standards; losers get relegated to the pack—regardless of their status under the old paradigm. IBM's System/360 family was such a fundamental advance.

After IBM established its control over the leading mainframe architecture in the mid-1960s, it relegated its competitors to supplying peripheral equipment and, later, clones that conformed to its specifications. Competitors could not market a new product line until IBM had introduced its own, lest their products be incompatible with IBM's. IBM's competitors were always racing to reverse-engineer IBM products as they became available, but by the time plug-compatible products appeared, IBM was ready to move on to the next incremental advance on its own systems. IBM understood this game well and played it superbly for more than two decades—making itself synonymous with large-scale computing in the process.

Once IBM got on top, however, its managers became complacent. They began to confuse control over mainframe architecture with control over their customers. Their collective worldview of computing was shaped by decades of thinking that an IBM machine was fundamentally a large centralized system. New approaches that fell outside this ambit were either not worthy of contemplation or were fumbled when IBM attempted them. And so when innovations with potential to reconfigure the dominant IT architecture began to appear in the mid- and late 1970s, IBM management failed to understand the implications. They could not look beyond the established business system as Tom Watson, Jr., had when he brought component manufacture of the System/360 in-house to beat out GE and RCA. His successors were stuck with success.

IBM's difficulty in tackling the minicomputer should have alerted its top executives to the troubles IBM might soon face—but it did not. After its first rush of success, the minicomputer became a specialty product, and eventually, IBM produced the AS 400, which swept to the top of this niche in the mid-1980s.

No doubt, Apple Computer's microcomputer appeared at first to be another specialty product with only limited appeal to IBM's key corporate accounts. IBM management concluded that it could be ignored. When Frank Cary courageously disagreed with this viewpoint and established the skunkworks that gave IBM its personal computer, neither he nor the others on the CMC fully grasped the importance of keeping control over all aspects of the PC's technology. IBM management would never have tolerated opening up its mainframe design to outsiders, but they were less concerned about the personal computer. And so IBM used a computer chip from Intel and an operating system from Microsoft and in the process gave away control of the leading-edge product of the future.

IBM's initial failure to control PC architecture and secure rights to DOS, the personal computer operating system, may have been understandable at the time. The decision was made during the extraordinary rush to get the first IBM personal computer to market and at a time when IBM did not want to do anything that might adversely affect the outcome of its ongoing antitrust battle with the Justice Department. But once the personal computer came into its own, the failure to secure the rights to DOS or to develop a viable alternative was a serious management mistake.[1]

Why did this error occur? Partly because most of IBM's executives came from the mainframe business and didn't see a major role for personal computers. Partly because of poor judgment. It remains astonishing today that IBM executives ever forgot the lessons of the mainframe. This is the failing of IBM management that has most undermined its performance in recent years.

## A LOSS OF NERVE

The other great failing of senior management at IBM can be laid to a timidity in the marketplace that contrasted with the aggressiveness of the 1960s and early 1970s. The loss of nerve in the management committee can be traced back to a key failure—the F/S, or Future System. IBM had introduced System/370 mainframes in 1972, just as the U.S. economy went into recession. Alarmed by flat sales and predictions of lower future revenues due to rapid decline of computing costs in its mainframe business (an area of IT in which management's vision was remarkably acute), IBM rapidly embarked on an expensive project to change the direction of computing technology and the shape of the markets. The project, Future Systems, was handled like the System/360, as a tightly controlled, companywide attempt to advance information technology on many fronts. Had it succeeded, it might have had the same positive effect on IBM as did System/360. More importantly, it might have entrenched regular cannibalization—even of key products—as the only way to stay on top of the information-technology market.

F/S was overly ambitious for its time, however, and failed miserably, with unfortunate consequences at IBM. The candor and controversy that had been a feature of IBM's culture disappeared and a new reluctance to advocate change emerged. IBM's technology and its culture simultaneously became fixed for decades ahead. A second consequence was that division executives began to put the welfare of their own organizations above that of the corporation as a whole. This manifested itself most importantly in the resistance of the mainframe division to the introduction of new technology that might damage sales of its products. This was a crucial issue for a company in the fast-moving information-technology industry. From the ruins of F/S came the mainframe-myopia that so severely damaged IBM in the 1990s.

In the past, IBM managers had sometimes shied away from cannibalizing their own products, but the chief executives had compelled the changes. Examples include the transition from the still-profitable 1401 computers to System/360 and from System/360 to System/370. In the wake of the failure of F/S, however, IBM turned around. Power shifted from those committed to change to those with stakes in existing products, particularly the mainframe division.

The mainframe division had felt abused during the F/S effort because many of its engineers were tied up in F/S for the first half of the 1970s and missed one of the division's regular development cycles. The mainframe group subsequently did everything it could to protect its own interests, including using the failed F/S as a club whenever a bold developmental initiative was again proposed. Not only did IBM's most important division not undertake strategic technological initiatives, it opposed them in the corporation as a whole. Thus the shadow of the failed F/S project darkened the future of IBM.

The F/S project was damaging to IBM in another, possibly equally significant way. It is a classic example of generals trying to win the last war. The 360 had won the mainframe war for IBM, but in the 1970s when IBM was squandering research effort on F/S—another attempt to win the mainframe war—a new struggle was just beginning. Xerox already had a microcomputer in its California laboratory, and Steven Jobs and his associates were even then working on the first commercial micro, the foundation of Apple Computer. But IBM had no comparable effort. IBM, with the biggest research and development budget and best R&D facilities in the information-technology industry, should have foreseen the microcomputer and exploited its technology to develop the industry. But it did not.

When, finally, IBM did develop a microcomputer, the executives who brought it to fruition were as protective of their division's interests as were the mainframe executives of theirs. They did everything they could to protect their independence from headquarters. Thus the division producing the hardware central to the new technology that would replace mainframes also discouraged any corporate-level development initiative that might have moved IBM to a leadership position in the next technology phase, client-server computing.

IBM executives had bet the company on development of the 360, and had won. They did not intend to bet the company on the F/S, but almost did so. When the project failed, not only did it leave the company risk-averse in the future, but IBM missed the opportunity to break into leadership of the new computing paradigm. The mainframe and personal computer divisions played important roles in impeding internal efforts to commercialize Reduced Instruction Set Computing (RISC) technology, one of the more useful results of the F/S project. Despite its considerable merits, this new technology never found acceptance among IBM's entrenched interests; in a post-F/S environment, no one was willing to force its use on the product divisions. In 1986, Sun Microsystems introduced its RISC workstations and took the lead in an industry segment that grew to several billion dollars in revenue in just a few years. After realizing the market potential, IBM finally made a serious attempt at commercializing its own RISC technology and introduced its line of workstations in 1990—two decades after it had pioneered the technology.

An even more serious consequence of IBM's failure to embrace RISC technology than the loss of time may have been the missed opportunity to power mainframes with inexpensive RISC processors capable of higher performance at lower cost, thereby possibly avoiding the rout of its mainframe products in the early 1990s.

A further highly significant consequence of the F/S debacle was the decentralization of development programs, a seemingly rational response to a major failure. It appeared that information technology was fragmenting and that future advances would not be of the sweeping variety offered by an F/S or System/360 project. So a plethora of independent development efforts replaced the one large strategic initiative. Unfortunately, proliferation and decentralization of development resulted in top executives trying to manage a process, not a strategy. This was a subtle but crucial difference, and it had very unfortunate results for IBM.

It is not too much to blame F/S for much of what later went wrong in IBM: The failure of a major strategic initiative can well have an impact of this magnitude. After the battle of Stalingrad had been lost, Hitler met with his top command to plan Germany's next steps. His chief of staff seized the occasion to make one of his few comments critical of the Führer. "A strategic failure of this magnitude," he told the assembly, "can only be redeemed in the next war." Germany, he was saying, could not escape the consequences of the failure at Stalingrad—World War II had been lost. To redeem the disaster at Stalingrad, Germany would need a fresh start: the next war.

IBM could not escape the consequences of the failure of the F/S initiative. It would find an opportunity to redeem itself only in the next competitive war: after the collapse of the mainframe and the emergence of a new paradigm of information technology. That competitive war is, of course, the one now in progress.

Who is to blame for IBM's difficulty in adapting to the new generation of information technology? The answer is that blame must be assigned to those who pressed the F/S initiative in the 1970s and failed.

## OVERLY CENTRALIZED MANAGEMENT

The IBM that Tom Watson, Jr., passed on to Vin Learson in 1971 employed about 200,000 people (one-third of whom joined after the announcement of System/360 in 1963). Fifteen more years of growth under Frank Cary and John Opel gave the incoming CEO John Akers a work force that had doubled to more than 400,000 by 1985.

To direct 400,000 people in a top-down, highly centralized organizational structure—one that allowed little of the local autonomy used in many firms of similar size—was a complex task. Unfortunately, IBM's own executives apparently did not see the sluggishness with which the firm was responding to their ever-more-urgent memos to change. In effect, IBM had expanded itself into an ungainly giant in danger of slipping on every banana peel it encountered in the marketplace. The fragmenting information-technology markets kept supplying an increasing number of banana peels after the advent of the IBM PC in 1981, but that was almost incidental to the firm's ongoing woes. IBM might even have toppled of its own weight had technology not given it a push first.

IBM needed decentralization of operating decision-making and a centralized strategy for developing information technology. In large part because of F/S, IBM had developed the opposite—decentralization of strategic decision-making with a continuing large degree of centralization in operating decisions. Top executives lost sight of strategy while keeping too much operational decision-making; division executives sought strategic independence (which was of little use to them), while focusing on their own interests rather than those of the company as a whole.

The company was being managed from the center as a single business. Its most recent success had been the result of a centralized project—the System/360 and its 370 successor. But now there was no central strategic development initiative; instead, there was a morass of process management.

Many management analysts now urge executives to manage processes, not tasks or activities. In general, this is good advice. But there are exceptions. The basic technique in managing processes is to leave key decisions, including some strategic decisions, to lower-level managers who are closer to the marketplace in their particular product or service niches. That is, process management is appropriate for top executives in a decentralized business. It is not appropriate for a centralized business such as IBM was in the 1980s.

When IBM's top managers ceased to oversee the strategic direction of technology development, strategy was not left to semi-autonomous divisions—of which IBM had none—it simply disappeared from sight. The implications of this are profound. John Akers failed to see the changing direction of information technology in part because his predecessors had ceased to watch—in fact, they had taken the steps that kept him blind. No one on IBM's top management team was watching the strategic development of technology; they were too busy managing a process.

Had IBM been more decentralized—that is, had IBM's upper-middle-level managers been given more discretion—then process management in the development area would have been appropriate. But IBM was not decentralized, and process management from the top left the strategic aspects of technology unnoticed. Further, to monitor processes, management spawned a bewildering variety of procedures, and bureaucracy flourished. Strategy was lost, staff and review multiplied, and IBM became ever more costly and rigid.

## A GREAT TIDE

Assessments of the responsibility of IBM's top executives for what went wrong at the firm should be seen in an industry context. What IBM has gone through, all other computer companies have also experienced, with the possible exception of Hewlett-Packard. Industry fundamentals changed in the 1980s and early 1990s from high growth rates to little or no growth; from rentals to sales as the dominant form of customer exchange; from high profit margins on sales to much lower ones; and from few to very many competitors. These changes in the industry represented a very large tide shifting directions, and it swamped almost all the companies and their chief executives. John Akers left the industry in the early 1990s, but he wasn't alone. Ken Olsen at Digital also left as did John Scully at Apple, Rod Canon at Compac, and others.

Should we conclude then that IBM's difficulties and those of its senior executives were inevitable, part of a larger picture in which they were more victims than guilty parties? We are reluctant to do so. While traditional hardware manufacturers suffered, software firms and manufacturers such as Intel prospered. IBM certainly had the potential to shift toward software and prosper as well. This was the challenge for its top executives—one which they failed to meet.

## HOW IBM EXECUTIVES "AIMED" WRONG

The mnemonic AIM, short for Apple, Intel, and Microsoft, sums up the various mistakes of IBM senior executives. It was not so much that these three firms bested IBM in the marketplace as it was that they benefited from errors made by IBM's executives. In a sense, the AIM companies symbolize the failure of IBM's executives to capitalize on a shift in technology.

IBM's lack of contact with its customers allowed Apple to persuade IBM that the personal computer would find its primary market among home users; because of this conviction, IBM abandoned key elements of its sales and distribution approach in favor of methods for reaching retail customers. IBM later discovered that its sales of personal computers were overwhelmingly to businesses.

IBM's fear of antitrust prosecution caused it to cede the microprocessor in the general marketplace to Intel (for years IBM had been the largest producer of microprocessors, but made them solely for use in its own products). IBM's failure to see that market standards for personal computers would be set by software and not hardware led IBM to cede control over the personal computer operating system to Microsoft.

These errors were not made by the rank-and-file of IBM—they were made by IBM's top management. Had IBM's executives aggressively backed the personal computer, had they marketed an IBM version of the Intel microprocessor, and had they quickly displaced Microsoft's personal computer operating system, IBM's share price would never have taken the dive it did. And the company's traditional culture, with its emphasis on employment security, would have continued in place, to be admired throughout the business world.

## Chapter Nine

# IBM as a Victim of the Pundits

ONE OF the less conventional views of what went wrong at IBM concerns the fundamental changes taking place in the world's capital markets. Since the early 1980s, shareholders, particularly institutional ones, have become increasingly impatient and aggressive—just about the opposite of what IBM required of its financiers.[1] Wall Street has never really understood IBM, as evidenced by the wide swings in its share price. But this hasn't stopped pundits from telling IBM's executives how to run the business.

## CHANGES ON WALL STREET

In earlier decades, Wall Street accepted the proposition that a firm owed obligations to several types of stakeholders—among them shareholders, customers, suppliers, and employees—and further, that stockholders were entitled to only a fair return on their investment. Wall Street today champions the rights of shareholders above those of all other stakeholders. Investors have also become more myopic than in the past; they now heavily favor short-term results, preferring one-shot restructurings to orderly change (and related charges) spread over several years. Finally, Wall Street has developed a peculiar astigmatism with regard to the valuation of corporate assets; it no longer assigns much if any capital value to intangibles such as shared business culture or loyalty among employees, while strongly insisting that the costs associated with building such intangibles be charged immediately to the income statement rather than capitalized on the balance sheet with tangible assets like property, plant, and equipment.

These changes in Wall Street thinking are due in part to the chronic inflation of the 1970s. Inflation is a tax on investors; it first erodes the nominal value of investment returns and then embeds itself in the underlying term structure of interest rates. Wall Street has adopted analytic methods for coping with inflation, the most widely used of which is an adaptation of the *present-value* approach to investment decisions that reflects market interest rates—and thereby incorporates the so-called best available guess as to what future rates of inflation will be.[2] The modified present-value approach to investment decisions seems to be a straightforward response to an economic problem, but in applying the solution, Wall Street has created a short-term bias in investment behavior.

To illustrate the depth of the problem, consider the following calculation: A nominal interest rate of 16 percent sustained for ten years creates a present-value factor of 4.4 in the tenth year, making the expected value of a payment on the investment in that year less than one-quarter its nominal size when stated in present-value terms. And in the late 1970s, 16 percent was a common rate of return on publicly traded U.S. government debt. Private sector investments, which face payment uncertainties as well as inflationary expectations, had rates even higher than 16 percent per annum; investors developed correspondingly shorter investment horizons when evaluating them. Inflation thus turned the market into a trader's paradise—a relentless search for immediate returns through churning securities on short-term news and views. The market no longer performed its traditional function of raising patient capital to support long-term corporate growth strategies.

While inflation was providing a powerful impetus to shorten investment horizons, the U.S. capital markets were also experiencing a major change in institutional mechanics triggered by the development of computerized trading systems and a wide array of options and futures contracts (vehicles for managing financial risk) that have cut trading costs and greatly increased liquidity in the equity market. In the past, corporate finance was much more of a relationship game; with fewer hedging tools available to them, the bankers who raised capital, the investors who provided it, and the analysts who facilitated the transfer all tended to take a long-term view of an investment's prospects because they would be stuck with the results of their decisions for some time to come. Selling out of large positions was both costly and inconvenient. The leading investment houses acted more like merchant bankers than traders; they made bets and stuck with them. Investment bankers even found their way onto corporate boards.

Today, the institutional money managers who control most available equity capital through public mutual funds or private pension funds face far more liquid markets. With quarterly performance reporting and easy investor access to their money—with the exception of closed-end funds—these managers have tremendous incentive to favor short-term trading strategies; the old buy-and-hold approach to investing in equities does not appeal to impatient fund buyers. And so the analysts who support the fund managers must generate trading—as opposed to investment—data; the subtleties of long-term performance must be sacrificed to understanding current earnings prospects.[3]

## WHY WALL STREET MATTERS

The changes on Wall Street would not have much impact on IBM in the past. Although many analysts following the firm were not completely satisfied with it—especially its reluctance to lay off so-called excess employees—its market capitalization was large enough to protect it from them, and IBM's managers remained free to manage to the pulse of their firm's own internal rhythms—and did so.[4] Fund managers, "widows and orphans," and even loyal employees who purchased shares of the premier growth stock of the century when they were valued at about $51 each in mid-1979 saw their investment surge above $160 in the mid-1980s and then plunge to $40 in mid-1993.

With the recent changes at the top of IBM, however, a watershed has been reached; IBM's institutional shareholders have finally demonstrated their ability to reach the company's board of directors. The shift of power over company affairs to IBM's shareholders means that, much more so than in the past, they can influence IBM's future course—and Wall Street is sitting right at their elbows with its new found quarterly wisdom. What Wall Street thought suddenly mattered a great deal to IBM; after decades of being the darling of Wall Street, IBM became first its whipping boy and then its victim.

Partisans of capital-market discipline seem to imagine that investors will be essentially passive players in the internal management of companies, voting with their feet by buying shares of successful firms and selling shares of distressed companies. Investor representatives often go much further, however, espousing favored remedies for a corporation's renewal. In the early 1990s, the popular prescriptions for IBM were to downsize, delayer, and decentralize—and IBM listened, even though it may not have been in the firm's long-term interest.

## REVIEWING THE MOVEMENTS IN IBM's STOCK PRICE

IBM's stock price movement tells different stories when viewed from different perspectives. In nominal terms, IBM's stock price has gone through three major cycles in the past fifty years: first, a rise and decline from 1943 to 1974, interrupted by a brief drop just before the introduction of System/360 in 1964 (no doubt reflecting the company's internal turmoil); second, a sharp rise and decline from 1975 to 1981; and third, a rise and decline from 1982 to the present. Overall, Figure 9.1 shows a steady increase in stock prices for over forty years, followed by a sudden decline in the last few years.

IBM stock seems to have performed well in nominal terms until at least 1991, but when these prices are adjusted for inflation (see Figure

*Figure 9.1*   Nominal Prices for IBM Stocks (1943–1993)

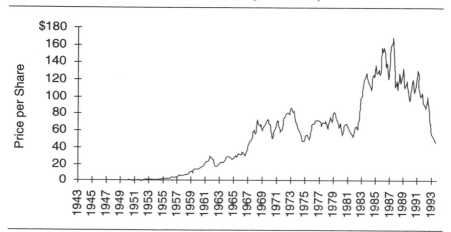

*Note:* Adjusted for splits.

9.2),[5] their movements can also be demarcated into three major cycles that coincide with those in Figure 9.1. The decline at the end of the first cycle, spanning 1973 and 1974, was much larger in magnitude than that of the past two years. Figure 9.2 thus reveals early growth with long-term decline over at least the twenty years following 1974, due partly to inflation.

Still another angle from which to view IBM's performance is to compare it to the performance of the broader market. When IBM's stock price is compared with the S&P 500 Index,[6] the cycles take somewhat different shapes (see Figure 9.3): first, a run-up from 1943 to 1961, followed by a dip to a slightly lower plateau; second, a broad rise and decline from 1965 to 1980, with several peaks and valleys obscuring the underlying trend; and third, a rapid rise and then a sharp dip from 1981 to the present. Figure 9.3 shows us a picture of a company that experienced strong growth, stagnated for almost twenty years, and is presently in decline.

Figure 9.4 is a compilation bringing together the three favorite measures for viewing stock performance: nominal value, inflation-adjusted value, and a comparison against a broad market index. As the reader will quickly observe, the three measures remained remarkably convergent in their valuation of the company until about 1973, when the first serious inflation of the 1970s began. Thereafter, the inflation-adjusted measure of IBM's stock value diverged sharply from the other

*Figure 9.2*   IBM Stock Prices Adjusted for Inflation (1943–1993)

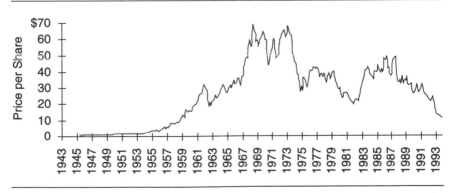

*Note:* Adjusted for splits.
CPI = 100 in 1967.

*Figure 9.3*    IBM Stock Prices Compared with the S&P 500 Index (1943–1993)

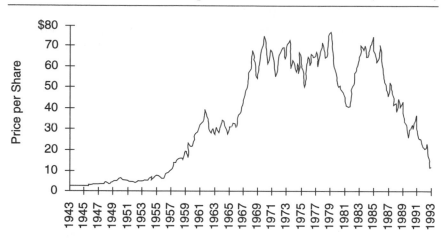

*Note:* Adjusted for splits.

*Figure 9.4*    Three Views of the Performance of IBM Stock Prices (1943–1993)

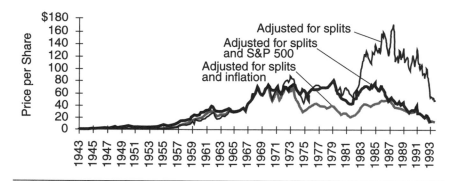

*Note:* CPI = 100 in 1967.

measures. In 1983, the S&P-weighted value of IBM's stock broke away from nominal value and headed downward to rejoin the inflation-weighted measure. Meanwhile, Wall Street was intent on pushing IBM's current price to a record high of about $180 per share in the late 1980s.

Figure 9.4 raises a number of interesting questions for Wall Street analysts and others to ponder. Why did the nominal, inflation-adjusted, and S&P-weighted share prices diverge so sharply in the late 1970s and 1980s? Did Wall Street inadvertently signal IBM's managers that they were doing the right thing even as the company was plunging into a short-term crisis? How could an entire community of analysts miss IBM's impending problems for five years, a period in which the nominal price of the stock kept soaring? The only rational answer is that the short-term, linear nature of market forecasting gave the analysts the answer that they were looking for. Today the linear trend points downward, and so the stock price is depressed even as the company recovers.

## AN ALTERNATIVE EXPLANATION FOR MOVEMENTS IN IBM's SHARE PRICE

The capital market's tendency toward short-term thinking and its astigmatism concerning organizational factors make it as perilous to suggest that IBM was fairly valued at $40 to $45 in mid-1993 as that it was fairly valued at $160 to $175 in 1986 or $51 in 1979. Great difficulties lie ahead for IBM's recovery unless investors understand more fully the long-term cycles that underpin the huge swings in market value demonstrated in the figures above.

Although IBM's fundamental strengths make it a marketing and service company, it is a technology-dependent enterprise. Such firms are captives of a cycle driven not by the ebb and flow of the financial markets, but by breakthroughs in basic science, product development efforts, and overall customer demand for the related technology. The process of innovation in science and technology does not make for orderly economics. Specific technologies do not always sell at sufficient margin over cost for a sufficient period of time to allow their developers to recover expenses, fund further research, and reward risk-takers—while better ideas wait obligingly in the wings. Instead, scientists and engineers may make major advances at any time, rendering highly profitable products obsolete overnight—whether development costs have been recovered or not.

To maintain profitability in such an uncertain environment, a firm must balance the harvesting of mature technology, which is subject to rapid obsolescence, with investment in new technology, which has not yet achieved market acceptance. This is neither painless nor easy and cannot be accomplished to the drumbeat of quarterly financial forecasts.

The history of the computer industry is littered with one-hit wonders that could not transcend the initial product that brought them prominence; even an IBM must be prepared to stop and regroup. When tabulators gave way to mainframes in the early 1950s, it took IBM ten years to rebuild market leadership over Remington Rand. When seamless migration across mainframes became important in the early 1960s, it took IBM nearly ten years to get System/360 going. When solid state circuits replaced vacuum tubes, it took IBM five years to push into component manufacture to block GE and RCA.

The effect of short-term market thinking on a firm that moves through multi-year cycles can be predicted in almost comic-opera fashion. Just as the market, blundering along in its short-term view, catches up to IBM, the company trips over the thresholds of changing organizational dynamics and falls behind again. This is illustrated in Figure 9.5.

In periods when IBM is shaking itself out of bureaucratic torpor, projected earnings will be uncertain and real growth neutral or nega-

*Figure 9.5*  A Cycles Approach to IBM's Stock Price

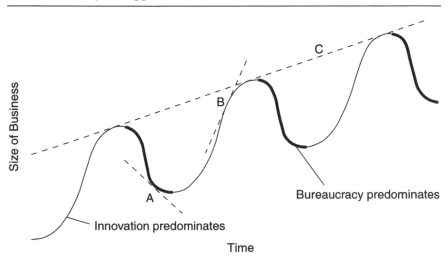

tive; the typical response of the equity markets would be to undervalue future potential and depress the stock below its true value; this is illustrated as A in Figure 9.5. In periods when IBM is pioneering new technology, projected earnings will be good and real growth positive; the markets therefore overvalue potential and elevate the stock above long-run equilibrium; this is illustrated as B in Figure 9.5. The real equilibrium is something approaching C in Figure 9.5, an upward sloping line that ignores short-term changes in earnings and prospects in favor of viewing the longer-term progress of the firm—however hair-raising this might be for institutional investors and their representatives.

## DECENTRALIZATION AND CUSTOMER RESPONSE

Investors in the early 1990s were understandably distressed by the decline in IBM's share price. If some investors took a long-term perspective, they went unheard among the clamor of those who wanted management to take immediate action to drive up the share price. A frequent recommendation was that the company be decentralized or broken up.

So John Akers began to decentralize IBM. In part, the intention was to improve responsiveness to customers by moving decision-making closer to the customer's point and time of request. In part, it was a response to outside criticism that became—via of IBM's board of directors—inside criticism.

IBM board members were repeatedly asked by members of other boards on which they sat how long they would tolerate IBM's mounting losses. As the company's distress continued, criticism mounted. "It doesn't take a rocket scientist to figure out that the parts of the business are worth more than the whole," one Wall Street analyst who asked not to be named told a reporter.[7]

The most common piece of unsolicited advice given to IBM's executives was that the company should be decentralized as a step toward major asset sales. Chief executive John Akers summed up the situation this way:

> In the mid-1980s we asked ourselves, "How well are we positioned?" Our answer: "Not well at all!" Our market strength was in large hardware, whereas the market growth was taking place in software, services, and

smaller machines (i.e., personal computers and workstations). Furthermore, we were organized around hardware, not markets, so we weren't
well set up to solve customer problems. It was clear that we needed to
change IBM and find ways to facilitate constant transformation.[8]

To respond to Wall Street's demands, Akers developed a new vision
of IBM, one that promoted greater flexibility. Akers had come to believe
that the root cause of IBM's problems was excessive size—that the firm
was unable to move fast enough to meet customer needs because
it had become too cumbersome to administer through a centralized
structure. And in December 1991, he decided to break the company up.
   Akers set in motion a reorganization plan intended to transform
IBM into a federation of thirteen smaller companies, nine manufacturing and development units and four marketing and service units. Major
changes in corporate policy accompanied the reorganization. Headquarters would no longer hold the units accountable for a "long list
of corporate-minded to-dos";[9] each subsidiary would negotiate a performance contract based on revenue, profit, cash flow, and return on
asset measures with IBM corporate. Each unit was freed to sell to any
customer; customers—not headquarters—were always to be the final
arbiter of what products or services IBM offered. To minimize coordination problems under the new plan, IBM also introduced market economics into its internal decision-making. The various business units
were to negotiate among themselves transfer prices for products that
reflected true market conditions, and subsidies based on eroding proprietary technologies were to be rooted out.
   The reorganization was intended to be much more than a make-
over; the integrated single business was to become a multi-business.
Its new business units were intended to be so independent that they
were even required to obtain agreement from the corporation to use
the IBM brand!
   In shifting the focus of managers toward localized operating units
and away from headquarters, Akers hoped to replace conformance
with performance, decision by committee with greater entrepreneur-
ship, and hierarchy with teamwork. He also hoped to see better customer service. The corporate marketing department even prepared a
mock dialogue stressing the virtues of smaller business units.

*Customer:* So what changes should I expect to see?

*IBM:* You'll see a leaner, more entrepreneurial IBM working with a variety of partners to bring technology to market faster. You'll work with IBMers empowered to take risks on your behalf and equipped with specialized skills and a deeper understanding of your business. And you'll reap the benefits of a quicker, more responsive organization based on our division into a federation of IBM companies. Some of these changes have been evolutionary, some have been radical.

*Customer:* The federation is obviously a radical step. What does it consist of?

*IBM:* Right now [1991], it consists of nine manufacturing and development business units—everything from mainframes to personal systems to software to printers—and four geographical marketing and services companies, including IBM–North America—the marketing and services organization serving the United States and Canada.

*Customer:* Why did you create the federation?

*IBM:* To make us quicker on our feet and to clarify accountability for results. As you know, IBM was noted for strong links between our business units and centralized control at corporate headquarters. This model diffused accountability and provided little flexibility, so we couldn't respond as rapidly as today's market demands.

*Customer:* So how do you expect your business units to operate now?

*IBM:* In our new model, we expect the manufacturing and development (M&D) companies in the federation to be first to market with the highest quality products at competitive cost. We expect our marketing and services (M&S) companies to be the premier vehicle for delivering services and systems to our customers, resulting in high levels of customer satisfaction and revenue growth.

*Customer:* I'm concerned about getting called on by all of your business units; for example, Pennant Systems.

*IBM:* We understand your concern, but this is one principle that hasn't changed—we will maintain a single face to the customer. Pennant Systems is somewhat of an exception based on a need for specialization. We have not invested in developing markets for intermediate and high-end printers as we should have in the past, and we now want to make an unambiguous investment in this area with leading-edge products and superior service. Pennant Systems will eventually manage a subset of IBM's field service force. These Pennant customer engineers will become experts in our customers' industries, applications, advanced function printing (AFP) software and other areas critical to rapid, high-quality printing and machine availability. However, Pennant Systems will be working through your IBM account team, which is responsible for packaging every facet of the solution we deliver.[10]

It all sounded very promising, but unforturnately it did not work out as expected. Instead, Akers had fallen into the same trap as Frank Cary had two decades earlier. IBM operates best as a single business, and 1993 was the worst year ever for its financial performance.

Many customers didn't at all experience the greater responsiveness that Akers intended to achieve. Instead, with decentralization, the occasionally noted lack of coordination among IBM's various units became more marked. "IBM divisions never worked toward the same goal," one customer complained in 1994. "They were working against each other."

Some customers now found their business parceled out among a number of IBM units, from none of which were they large enough to attract much attention. "We haven't seen an IBM rep in three years," said one former customer. "I've noticed a depreciation in the level of service from IBM," said another. "We used to see IBM's reps here on a regular basis. I haven't seen one around now for over a year." Observed a third, "We've found it harder to get things done with IBM. We have good rapport with local IBM people but, with the reorganization, it's made it difficult getting problems resolved and getting contact with the right people."

Ironically, some customers had exactly the opposite problem and were equally put off. "Consistency of service has diminished, and there's a great deal of confusion in the marketplace. These things exceed the benefits of dealing with IBM. I currently have four to five IBMers calling on me to sell me a box. Each one is selling a different box. I feel each one is trying to talk me into an inappropriate machine because that's the only thing that person can sell." The field sales force had not been formally divided among IBM's new subsidiaries and divisions. But there was no sales strategy outlining what should be offered to customers, resulting in confusion over what machines were to be sold by whom.

"IBM has been confusing as a vendor," commented another customer. "They've messed up their marketing direction. I receive multiple and competing contacts from within IBM. It's confusing for the customer. Some of this is chaos from the decentralization, but some of it is because they haven't gotten their marketing efforts organized. The restructuring is very confusing to me."

Little of IBM's marketing effort addressed the critical problem of new customers seeking less grand solutions to their computing problem at lower costs. "IBM dug its own grave in our company," explained an executive. "They were arrogant, unresponsive, extremely expensive, and overly bureaucratic. Basically, IBM didn't want to do business with us. They told us they wanted to focus their energy on major clients, and we weren't one of them. If you weren't spending millions, then you couldn't get IBM's attention."

What is remarkable about this is how unnecessary it was. If an IBM branch chose to devote its resources to larger clients, that was understandable. But to convey that decision directly to smaller clients and thereby alienate them was evidence of the arrogance for which the company has been so roundly condemned by its customers.

Other customers made related points. Said one, "Dealing with IBM has become more difficult. IBM used to provide total solutions. Now, we're dealing with competing units and you can't get the same service from one unit to the next. It's become very confusing." "IBM isn't the one-stop place it used to be to get answers to all of your questions," concluded an executive at one of IBM's larger customers. Said another, "The bottom line on IBM's demise is that it makes life more difficult and challenging for us. It's like when AT&T split up. IBM's decentralization has fostered more competition in the marketplace and caused buyers to be more sophisticated. Now instead of being a one hardware shop, we've gone to other vendors as well. Our buying patterns have changed. It's made the world more complicated for us."

None of this should suggest that all IBM customers have been adversely affected by the decentralization. Our survey found that 63 percent of firms dealing with IBM found no adverse affect. But of this group, 41 percent said that they did little business with IBM. Hence, of IBM's primary customers, about two-thirds report problems with decentralization (37 to 22 percent).

## THE GREAT MISTAKE

Under pressure from investors, John Akers had begun to break up IBM. His purpose in establishing a federation of companies was to make it easier to sell parts of the firm, if that became advisable. IBM had been one big system, with no independent financials for its various units. This had led to great difficulties when IBM sold its typewriter division. To avoid a similar situation in the event of another sale, decentralization was needed. Decentralization also promised to give the new units of the company greater automony in making product decisions.

Unfortunately, observers saw Akers's actions, perhaps wrongly, but understandably, as the first steps toward creating a number of fully integrated businesses with separate sales forces, a solution to IBM's woes that many analysts were urging on the company. So confusion developed about IBM's intentions, with many people both outside and inside the company concluding that Akers intended to let the market decide what it wanted to buy from IBM.

Probably in line with Akers's plans—but perceived as due to resistance by key sales executives—IBM never divided its field sales force among the newly established units. With the exception of a separate force for selling printers, IBM presented its customers with one face. Singleness was preserved.

Akers embraced the federation of companies less as a strategy than as a retreat from strategy. IBM had strong technology and a favorable product line, and it had a sales force ready to do the company's bidding. But what technology or product should be IBM's strategic orientation? What should IBM suggest that its customers buy?

Unable to decide on an answer and blind to customers' wishes because close relationships with them had been abandoned, Akers tried to let the market decide. IBM's chairman sought to sit above the fray, like General Electric's, and reward winners and losers.

This was Akers's great failure: to try to solve a problem of basic business strategy through an organizational route. Akers's overly ambitious expansion had put the company into difficulty. He'd tried to resolve it by using the field sales force to push product out of his factories onto his customers, but it hadn't worked because the customers' information needs were changing. Failing to correct his strategy, Akers instead decided to break up his company and let the market decide. Even though this course was pressed upon him by investor representatives and industry pundits, it was the wrong approach.

## HOW WALL STREET MAY BE DESTROYING IBM AND COMPANIES LIKE IT

What sustains technology firms during the downturns in their business? Products become obsolete before commercially viable replacements are in sight; bureaucratic infighting over new directions in markets and technology intensifies; managers who've grown fat on past success, nearing retirement, are most unwilling to change. The answer is a strong competitive culture.

Culture is crucial because of the fundamental nature of technology-dependent firms. Much of the value of such firms is bound up in its people and their willingness to keep working with customers and managers through the turmoil of reinvention—while old technology and infrastructure are torn down and replaced.

Capital markets that assign little value to the social contract binding employees to a company in hard times—while at the same time penalizing the firm for the liabilities it incurs in good times to maintain the basic policies that sustain that social contract—run the risk of destroying the basis for long-term performance. If a company must weaken its culture to please the markets in the short term, it will not be able to deliver greater performance in the long term. The best employees will either depart for greener pastures when their pay and perks are put in jeopardy, or they will have assumed that they must look out for themselves and never join such a firm in the first place.

What if IBM had been left alone by the markets after 1990? It would have maintained its course and endured some losses as it tried to reposition and reorient itself in a changing industry.

But since IBM was not insulated from Wall Street's advice, its executives lost confidence in their long-term strategy and bowed to Wall Street's wishes, accepting record restructuring charges to make rapid short-term changes.[11] Wall Street in the 1990s broke the concentration of IBM's management on the technology cycle—something it had been unable to do in 1950, when the tabulator technology was dying; or in 1961 to 1963, when migration between different-sized mainframes was becoming critical, and Thomas J. Watson, Jr., had to run to his investors with a rights issue to prevent IBM from going technically bankrupt; or even in 1969, when the 360 was aging.

The very size of IBM's restructuring charges has had a strong impact on the company's business. Surprised customers have questioned whether they should continue purchasing mainframes and looking to IBM for direction. Unsettled employees have lost the confidence they once had in IBM and in their own job performance. Most importantly, the charges disrupted IBM's long-term view of the marketplace and its technology cycles.

Much of IBM's top management in the 1985 to 1993 period had been in the firm during the System/360 crisis. It is hard to believe that they did not know how to cannibalize a profitable product; it is easier to believe that they understood how messy and uncertain the process could be. This may explain why they resisted cannibalization of the mainframe until the last moment instead of beginning it in the mid-1980s, when it might still have been possible to make the transition while keeping IBM in the black. But once IBM's management began dancing to the market's tune, responding to quarterly pressure for results with decentralization and abandonment of such practices as full employment, its problems only worsened.

A capital market that fails to understand the fragile nature of the employee base on which IBM relies to sustain it through the turbulence of transition and that mindlessly pressures IBM into rapid-fire actions unsuited to its organizational cycle may end up pushing IBM into bankruptcy. A firm that survived at least seven decades by largely ignoring capital markets may meet its demise as a result of finally acceding to their demands.

# PROSPECTS FOR CHANGE

# Trying to Transform IBM's Corporate Culture

IN 1986, IBM began to reinvent itself. By then it was clear that the firm's aspiration to have $100 billion in revenues by 1990 would not be fulfilled. It was also becoming increasingly evident that its position in information technology was slipping. A new generation of technology was emerging, built around networks of microcomputers, and IBM wasn't in the lead.

Needing to reposition itself in the marketplace, IBM began to change some of the provisions in its unwritten contract with its employees. The firm could no longer afford to provide all of the benefits to which its employees had become accustomed.

To restore profitability, IBM tried to put itself on a new fiscal regime. Productivity became more important than fairness, which at IBM had always meant rewarding individual performance. IBM began reducing its work force through selective attrition, targeting for voluntary retirement or severance initiatives workers in jobs deemed least essential to the firm's future, regardless of individual performance. Efficiency also demanded finding ways to lower compensation paid per unit of output, specifically through the use of variable compensation and bonuses rather than large fixed pay and benefit packages.

## DECENTRALIZING COMPENSATION

In the past, IBM had seen itself as a single business marketing information-technology systems and services to large corporate clients. The firm also had centralized personnel administration; respect for the individual dictated that job evaluation, classification, and salary benchmarking be done by a corporate personnel staff to ensure that equal work received equal pay throughout the firm. In some locations, IBM paid above prevailing wage levels; in others, IBM paid below prevailing wage levels. But every employee knew, within broad limits, that all IBMers earned the same pay for the same work.

A philosophy of internal pay equity reinforced by one underlying set of terms and conditions served IBM well when it was selling large proprietary computers to a select group of big customers. But when the market for information services fragmented with the arrival of the microcomputer, the old standard terms and conditions no longer fit all of the niches in which IBM chose to play. Marketing mainframes is in many ways a different business than marketing microcomputer networks; the clients and the skills are not the same.

As IBM struggled with financial losses, it decided it must adapt itself to the changing marketplace by devolving authority over employment terms to operating units. This meant that IBM would no longer have one social contract but many, reflecting the economic diversity of its different business units. Decentralization was intended to help managers run their units more effectively. Localized social contracts allowed wages to respond directly to local conditions; for example, IBM reduced the powers of central management in the process of empowering managers in their own business segments.

## CHANGING THE MEANING OF PAY FOR PERFORMANCE

Pay and benefits at IBM underwent complex changes as the firm attempted to cut overall compensation while increasing the amount of work generated per dollar spent. These changes fell under the rubric of pay for performance, although they had much broader implications than the term usually encompasses.

In the early 1980s, IBM had been relying heavily on the general goodwill of the firm's employees to motivate performance. Watson, Sr., had understood that he could not motivate with non-variable pay only—IBM used sales commissions—but he wanted stability among non-sales employees and so stressed employee participation over pay differences as a primary employee reward.

The problems of relying on goodwill were apparent in the workings of the performance appraisal system. It had originally been conceived as a tool for *individual* performance, planning, and measurement. Employees had separate performance plans; everyone could make a plan—or not. Managers could not measure relative contributions by different employees; they could only rate individuals against themselves. The consequence was that marginal performers remained in the company. Truly bad performers who failed to make plan year after year could be dismissed, but nothing could be done about the marginal performer who always seemed barely to make plan. As long as satisfactory ratings were maintained, marginal performers had to be kept on, even though they took salary dollars that might have been spent on superior performers. Eventually, IBM did introduce changes that allow it to identify and dismiss marginal employees.

Today's information industry demands innovation, creativity, and teamwork. Fluctuating margins and volatile customers make attention to business performance essential, but a pay system that emphasizes measurement of individual achievement and intrinsic rewards and offers no strong short-term incentives cannot drive superior business performance under these conditions. Some competition for jobs had to be induced, so IBM moved toward pay for performance backed up by a new set of performance measurement criteria that emphasized ranking. Performance standards were steadily raised.

IBM altered its practices because the incentives flowing from the existing compensation plans no longer met its business needs. Salaries and predictable bonuses were not motivating top performance. IBM corporate executives decided that variable pay motivates; fixed pay scales do not.

IBM had always tried to pay employees for individual performance. Salespeople were paid on commission; other employees received salary increases reflecting their own long-term performance. But in trying to turn the company around, top management gave the phrase *pay for performance* a different connotation in the company. Pay for performance now meant not simply a supervisor's evaluation of an employee's performance but actual, measurable contributions to IBM's success.

IBM no longer relied solely on the positive motivation arising from employee loyalty to the company; it began to use whatever leverage it could gain from varying compensation *and* recognition. Individual performance ratings were adjusted to incorporate a rising minimum acceptable performance standard; what was acceptable last year might become grounds for performance-related termination the next year. In addition, ranking was introduced so that managers could measure employees' relative contributions to the business with the aim of identifying and targeting the poorest performers in every unit for outplacement, regardless of their specific achievement against a performance plan.

To increase the motivating power of the compensation package as a whole, the relative weight of fixed salary was reduced and variable bonuses driven by business performance were increased. New bonuses supplementing the existing merit pay plan were tied to formal revenue and profit targets; the practice of negotiating bonuses after the year's results were known was dropped. Incentives for managers range from 15 percent to 75 percent of base salary; many plans carry a 10 percent bonus for achieving 100 percent of performance plan, plus 3 percent for each 1 percent over plan (capped at 200 percent of base pay). Underperformance triggers penalties, a loss of 2 percent of projected bonus for each 1 percent that performance falls below 90 percent of the target amount. People in units that do well now earn more than before, while people in units that do poorly earn less.

In addition, the global level of compensation was reduced through selected benefit cuts. Both pension and health care benefits were modified to contain open-ended costs. For example, IBM embraced managed health care; capped contributions to its pension plan at thirty years; and abolished vacation-pay banking, a practice in which employees had accumulated paid vacation days until they could take off a large block of time—sometimes several years off prior to retirement—at full pay.

Employees were still offered reassignment if their jobs were declared surplus, but severance packages for the thousands who were leaving were reduced to the minimums required by law. The change was dramatic. In 1985, when IBM closed its facility at Greencastle, Indiana, employees leaving the company received two years' severance pay and an allowance for additional training and education. Five years later, employees whose facilities were closed received much less.

Why were these changes introduced? The old compensation system had served IBM well when the underlying operational objective was to ensure the consistent execution of key tasks. For years IBM had won in the marketplace not through innovation but by providing the same high-quality products and service to clients. Consistent behavior toward customers came from experience and socialization in IBM's culture. Such reliability could only be developed through long tenure; thus the firm sought to retain employees until they retired. To prevent disruptions in employees' consistent execution of their jobs caused by preoccupation with wide pay variations among workers, IBM tilted its reward system toward fixed and long-term compensation; within job categories everybody received basically the same pay, with small differences for extraordinary merit or performance.

The merit-pay component of salary was cumulative over time; never more than a small percentage of total pay to preserve harmony in the performance evaluation process, it was awarded to no more than a tiny minority of employees each year. Base pay increased through promotions, scheduled for every two or three years. To this base pay, IBM added benefits contingent on continued employment, but then further reduced variability by making most people's long-term benefits fixed through the full employment practice.

The old system was difficult to change. An analysis done by IBM staff in 1992 found that about 30 percent of IBM's total compensation budget was spent on fixed salary; 35 percent on fixed benefits; 20 percent on working conditions and programs such as training; and only 15 percent on variable compensation, awards, and bonuses.[1] At a time when the firm was attempting to shift strongly toward variable compensation, this was a surprisingly low proportion. The same study revealed that every year about 1 percent of IBM's non-sales employees lost their jobs due to poor performance. IBM's full-employment practice protected the positions of everyone else—99 percent of the company's employees. They kept moving inexorably toward retirement at a substantial rate of pay.

Not surprisingly, risk-taking and innovation were unusual at IBM. No employee wanted to challenge a manager's approach to doing things. The managers controlled each employee's performance appraisal, which in turn determined an employee's benefits, salary, and pension.

## REDIRECTING TRAINING

Other aspects of IBM's personnel system came in for changes. In the late 1980s, IBM was spending more than $1 billion per year on training, with additional funds committed to Open Door and employee attitude surveys. IBM even went so far as to require forty hours of training per person per year. Was this expenditure needed?

It is often argued that a firm should spend considerable sums on training, since better skills will reduce waste, increase quality, or improve morale, effects that, over time, more than recoup the initial cost of the training. But unfortunately, far too many IBM employees saw the required training as a burden; it was not a motivator to them.

In the case of grievance programs like Open Door, the impact on motivation was equally invidious. IBM spent millions of dollars processing complaints, but was this money seen by employees as a benefit? When first established, IBM's grievance program stood out in the minds of employees who saw instances of arbitrary treatment in other firms. But legal precedents and common sense subsequently spread IBM-like practices to other firms; as a result the differential in treatment at IBM has been reduced.

To deal with this situation, IBM introduced the concept of total compensation. The firm tried to convey to its employees how little competitors paid for grievances and training, in order to draw attention to IBM's own more generous spending.

IBM also targeted its training program to generate more value for the firm. One of IBM's key assumptions about human resources had been that skills—not people—became obsolete. This belief drove training efforts in the 1980s: IBM spent billions to remake IBMers for new careers as their old jobs became redundant. But the emergence of new technologies made retraining and redeployment objectives increasingly difficult to attain. Much expertise was simply not transferable between mainframes and microcomputers; experience with the new technology became critical to subsequent employment success.

By the early 1990s, IBM was abandoning the full employment practice. But without a goal of lifetime employment, why should IBM invest in retraining people? Rather than retrain and redeploy displaced workers, IBM now found it cheaper to let them go and to hire from outside the firm whatever additional skills were needed.

No longer needing to retrain people for redeployment, IBM increasingly targeted its training programs not at giving employees new skills but at indoctrinating them with the culture changes necessary to sustain the firm in the long term.

## CULTURE CHANGE

Watson, Sr., tried from the beginning to make employees feel as though they were the firm to their customers, and there was always much paternalism in the culture. Although managers respected the employees, they retained full authority over them, and the firm itself was ruled by a strongly centralized management structure. At one time, Watson had fifty people reporting directly to him, although later chief executives had much smaller executive teams. As IBM expanded in size, it tried to decentralize, but it always seemed to remain centralized as top-down pressure outran the effective delegation of authority.

In the late 1980s, IBM along with most other large U.S.–based firms adopted a total quality management program; at IBM it was called Market-Driven Quality (MDQ). The notion was that improved quality should be seen, not from IBM's point of view, but from that of its customers—hence *market*-driven quality.

Experience with quality circles and other techniques has shown that quality improvement programs like MDQ require three elements for success: changes in work methods and equipment; training; and the freedom for employees to apply these new tools in the workplace. Freedom is often the missing link; without it, quality improvement becomes an management-led effort in which workers are pressed to change work patterns without their consent. For an MDQ program to work at IBM, the executives in charge realized, it had to be given a bottom-up flavor; employees had to have a real say in how their work was to be done, not just polled on their feelings toward management. This was the wellspring of a cultural revolution at IBM.

IBM came to MDQ after complex analysis of some basic problems, including products coming late to market and much higher than expected or desired defect rates. Studies showed that there were no technical failings responsible. IBM had the tools to address quality problems; what it lacked was the organization to put these tools to work.

Products were late to market because the designs were held up as people in marketing and R&D bickered over features. Costs were high because designs were rushed into production late and were shipped with mistakes that had to be reworked in the field. Finally, many employees were no longer thinking about their customers; they were focusing on internal controversies.

In retrospect, the cause of these difficulties is apparent: They were a result of the environment in which IBM had developed. For example, IBM's emphasis on consensus management had developed to ensure that basic issues in the design, manufacturing, and marketing of highly complex computers were raised and resolved *before* the machines went to market. When IBM built only a few thousand of each machine and customers relied on fault-free performance, everything had to be perfect and IBM needed a process to make sure that it was.

The penalty for seeking consensus was laggard implementation; consensus was thorough, but slow as a decision-making process. As marketplace competition increased with the arrival of the microcomputer, IBM was caught flat-footed. Technology began evolving so rapidly that IBM no longer had years to get a product right; adaptability, flexibility, and speed were critical to success in an open-systems world. IBM needed teamwork; it could no longer afford to have departments formally disputing one another until consensus was reached.

MDQ thus entailed a major cultural change at IBM. For quality to improve, the firm needed more teamwork, which required that employees be able to make decisions and act on their own. IBM had to use less hands-on management, train employees to work in teams, and give employees and managers incentives to change their existing behavior. Creating these incentives meant dismantling much of the existing centralized top-down management style. MDQ was neither sloganeering nor exhortation but an attempt to rebuild IBM.

It was clear from the beginning that MDQ would demand considerable training at several levels. First, employees and managers had to be told *why* they were being asked to change. Second, new skills and behavior had to be instilled. Knowledge about quality-process charts, benchmarking, and process measurement had to be imparted to each employee; skills like team-building had to be taught to managers.

A wide variety of media were used to drive home the message. Brochures, programs on IBM's internal television network, and videotapes for management presentations at department meetings were all prepared on the same basic theme: IBM must change because of competitive pressures and developments in technology. The message continued, describing the features of the new IBM: a delayered, more flexible, team-oriented work environment, with much less top-down direction and control and more employee initiative in working with customers. Exhibits 10.1 and 10.2 were among the materials prepared by IBM to explain to employees the changes being made.

The transformation envisioned was revolutionary. IBM had been one of the most centrally directed companies in the United States.

*Exhibit 10.1*   Transforming IBM

| From | To |
| --- | --- |
| Manage | Delegate/Lead |
| Control | Ownership/Participation |
| Direct | Empower |
| Employees as cost | Employees as asset |
| Information management-owned | Information shared |
| Hierarchical organization | Flatter organization |
| Risk avoidance | Risk management |
| Individual contributions | Team contributions |

*Exhibit 10.2*   Proposed Changes

| Culture Changes | Skill Changes |
| --- | --- |
| Customer as final arbiter | Leadership |
| Flatter organization | Empowerment |
| Shared information | Team-building |
| Risk management | Participation |
| Employee ownership | Risk management |
| Team contributions | Change management |

General Electric recruiters, for example, when persuading young managers to come to GE rather than go to IBM, would say that GE managers had substantial decision-making authority while at IBM managers simply carried out instructions from top executives. Jokes about life at IBM reinforced the point: "How long does an IBM manager have after something unusual happens before he or she calls corporate headquarters?" The answer: "A microsecond." Yet in the transformation now planned for IBM, managers were to direct less and delegate more.

IBM had been one of the most secretive of business organizations, with a healthy need-to-know principle. An employee wanting to learn about developments elsewhere in IBM had to demonstrate that the information sought was necessary in the performance of his or her job. Otherwise, the information wasn't available. The company had a number of security classifications, including "Confidential" and the more restrictive "IBM Confidential." Yet in the new IBM, managers and employees were to freely share information.

Finally, IBM had been among the firms most sensitive to its employees as individuals. Following the prescription set by Thomas J. Watson, Sr., of respect for the individual, IBM managers had been expected to pay close attention to each person who reported to them. Each IBMer was to have a close relationship with his or her supervisor; teamwork was much less important. IBM had been a collection of individuals working under close supervision to achieve common purposes as defined by top executives. Now it was supposed to become a collection of teams carrying out loosely defined missions.

With the new culture came a whole new set of skills, perhaps the most significant of which was to learn how to work effectively in teams. IBM's employees were understandably much concerned about becoming lost in a mass and invisible to their supervisors and to the firm as a whole.

But IBM's top executives were serious about attempting the transformation and utilized the strongest managerial levers to achieve it. Further refinements in the personnel system reinforced the message of change. Performance appraisal was the best communications vehicle at IBM; employees could ignore everything except their performance plans without the risk of being fired. Hence, by changing performance appraisal measurement criteria, the company transmitted new corporate objectives directly to employees. This linkage gave performance appraisal a major role in the MDQ process.

In particular, MDQ objectives were added to performance appraisal planning. All performance plans now included MDQ goals and objectives. For example, employees were required to identify their customers and focus on meeting customer requirements, and they had to improve their responses to customers' needs. Managers were required to adopt the new management style, incorporate team objectives into their thinking, and enhance employee decision-making.

MDQ terms and outcomes were also added to performance categories. As a result, managers rated superior created customer satisfaction, effective teamwork, and positive leadership—each an objective of the MDQ process.

The changes caused tremendous confusion, however. Empowerment meant that employees should be able to decide and act on business issues, not simply pass them up to managers for resolution. But how much discretion were employees to exercise? One internal document cautioned employees against taking empowerment too far. It read in part, "Empowerment does not mean that you are now free to redefine IBM's basic business goals."

IBM was struggling to be market-driven, that is, to be more responsive to customers. But how far was an IBMer to go in satisfying customers? IBM executives were soon urging employees to be careful not to go to far. "A good empowered decision," read a letter to IBM's employees, "is not only fair to the customer, but fair to IBM as well, taking into account our costs and need to be profitable."

## THE RESULTS OF IBM's EFFORTS

What was IBM's experience in modifying its social contract? Does it suggest that social engineering is in fact a costly exercise in frustration? Or, is it a vital management process?

IBM experiences teaches that, having created a social contract over many decades, a firm *can* modify its provisions. There is still life at IBM after the abolition of full employment! It is important to remember, however, that transformation of a social contract in ways viewed by employees as damaging to their interests can damage a firm. Fundamental changes must be carried out in an appropriate manner over an appropriate period of time.

Because social contracts take shape as employer and employees jointly refine contract provisions they find mutually useful, events from a firm's early history assume disproportionate influence, making the social contract rigid and difficult to change. Also, the strength of the social contract and the success of the firm are locked in a feedback loop. IBM's experience shows that a successful firm will attract employees comfortable with its social contract. As the social contract gains strength, the firm may appeal only to that type of employee. IBM attracted employees with an interest in security; when it decreased security, employees were demoralized.

Thus it was that IBM, under its new chief executive, Louis V. Gerstner, Jr., began its recovery efforts with an abandoned social contract, confusion over its replacement, and a demoralized workforce. This situation cast a long shadow over the company's future, but just how long remains uncertain.

## Chapter Eleven

# The Future of IBM

ON APRIL 1, 1993, Louis V. Gerstner, Jr., assumed the chairmanship of IBM, the first non-IBMer in the history of the company to ascend to the top job. The company was finally ready to jettison an aging technology and to embrace the emerging one. This is IBM's time-honored, though never routine, pattern of change. One leader, steeped in the success of an older generation of computer technology, finds it difficult to commit the corporation fully to cannibalizing the old to let the new flourish. He has to be replaced in a palace revolution by someone new—a person able to institute dramatic change.

In a company that measures, quantifies, and systematizes everything else, why does such an emotional, messy, and essentially human process continue decade after decade? The answer must lie with the chief executives themselves. They may be unwilling or unable to see the promise of new technology, lacking the vision to perceive its benefits for IBM and its customers. They may seek to avoid the turmoil that transition from one generation of technology to another creates in a company the size of IBM. Whether by resignation, retirement, or more recently, layoff, thousands of loyal IBMers, wedded by skill or inclination to the old technology, must leave the firm. And despite IBM's reputation for managing its earnings, such transitions from old to new cannot be made without financial reverses. No chief executive officer can face with equanimity the shrieks of investors, the projections of ruin for the company, and the criticism of lower management that inevitably accompany a decline in a firm's fortunes, however temporary.

John Akers had faced an even worse situation than had his predecessors. Wall Street in the 1990s was far less tolerant of earnings reversals, far less willing to look to the long term than it had been in the past. Computer companies reporting less than projected earnings encountered drastic declines in market value—slides of one-third of value in a single day's trading were not uncommon. When Wall Street recognized the end of the mainframe era, IBM's share price began a relentless decline that bottomed out at a loss of three-quarters of its previous value. No wonder Akers hesitated on the brink of the transition.

A new chairperson was required to wrench the company from its ties, nostalgic though they had become, to the old paradigm of computing. So Akers went, and Lou Gerstner came. IBMers at all levels expected Gerstner to bring change, and so he has.

IBM's transition to the new modes of computing is now under way. In 1994, nearly half of the company's hardware sales came from products introduced in the previous eighteen months. Since then, the pace of new product introductions has increased. For example, IBM introduced new software products to support electronic mail and group scheduling functions, much like Microsoft's *Exchange*. Some of IBM's newest products have come from Lotus Development Company, which IBM acquired in 1995; others were developed at IBM. The aim, IBM has said, is less to compete with *Exchange* than to give IBM's mainframe customers an easier migration path to client-server computing. The mainframe is not dead, but it is no longer dominant. It must be made to fit into the client-server architecture, in which today's massive databases ensure a role for mainframe servers. Big Blue is finally placing its mainframe product within the proper context for its customers' needs.

The company has begun a whole-hearted transition to the new paradigm of computing, freely cannibalizing its outdated technology. IBM's vast resources—human, physical, and financial—have been enlisted in this effort. IBM's revenues remain more than three times those of its nearest rival, Fujitsu, and more than four times those of third-place NEC. Microsoft and Intel combined have less than one-ninth the revenues of IBM.

IBM dominates many information-technology product markets. IBM leads seven of nine categories (sometimes by substantial margins), according to *Datamation,* an industry publication.[1] Of the remaining two categories, IBM is second in one and third in the other. Surprisingly, IBM has a larger market share in software than in large-scale mainframe systems. Although it leads in market share in most industry segments, however, IBM lacks a dominant position in any (its market share being generally in the 10 to 30 percent range). But IBM has a serious weakness in a key technology of the future—workstations. In this technology, IBM has little more than one-tenth the market, and lags well behind market leader Sun Microsystems.

For all of its massive revenues, IBM's strength is in the wrong products for a changing information-technology marketplace. IBM's industry-leading software, peripheral, and maintenance/services revenues are tightly tied to IBM's increasingly shopworn proprietary large-scale systems; without the hardware hook, its follow-on peripherals and software do not sell.

Information-services managers, who must set information-technology purchasing budgets, continue to move toward distributed computing and away from centralized systems. As they do so, their need for mainframe and mid-sized computers—and related software, services, and other products—shrinks. The margins that IBM can earn in these product categories are fading. Meanwhile, the firm lags badly in both market share and revenue in workstations, data communications, and other products essential to distributed computing; its temporary strength in microcomputers—marked by an 80 percent share in 1983—is now down to 17 percent in the *Datamation* survey and still dropping.[2] Meanwhile, the shift toward client-server computing has provided firms like Intel and Microsoft with a steady profit surge to invest in maintaining and expanding their technological lead over IBM.

The new generation of computer firms uses technology to much greater advantage in their own operations than IBM ever did. Their basic organizational structures, incentive programs, and management styles are all patterned after the emerging personal-computer networks, which allow tremendous flexibility, initiative, and fast reactions to customers. Salespeople can now put customers in direct communication with the engineers who wrote the software or designed the box the customer is looking at, sometimes while the sales meeting is still going on! IBM still uses the old system in which salespeople try to answer customers' questions based on their training or by inquiring up a chain of command. It is essential that the old sales system give way to the new, just as the old computing paradigm must give way to the new. IBM is moving slowly in this direction.

IBM is also repositioning itself to offer consulting and services. These areas may become the core of the new IBM. In the late 1980s, George Conrades, the first president of IBM–USA, created what became ISSC (Information Systems Solutions Corporation), taking IBM's first contract to do a customer's data processing. He also hired IBM's first consultant: There are now about one thousand. These steps allow IBM to help its customers integrate the elements of the new technological paradigm.

Despite these promising moves, the possibility is that technology integration will depend less on service (with its high overhead costs) and more on smart software and additional technology. These areas may be greater sources of value than having a provider that can link various pieces. If this proves to be the case, IBM will have greater than anticipated difficulties in the new market.

Most businesspersons—excluding information-technology professionals in American business (as we shall see below)—consider that Bill Gates of Microsoft has wrested the mantle of industry leadership from IBM. The informed general manager believes that Gates sees the future more clearly than does IBM. Reflecting Gates's orientation, discussions in the United States about information technology focus on the next technological wonder. This contrasts with IBM's business-oriented interest in the next major application of technology to a business process. Can IBM regain leadership?

Investors seem to think so. The company's share price has more than doubled from its low. To a large degree, this reflects an upsurge in the company's profitability. Cost-cutting has carried the share price up as cost savings went directly into profits. But sales remain subbornly stagnant. If the share price is to continue to improve, the company must put itself once again on a path of growth.

Renewed growth will require tremendous effort. The company has done itself substantial damage by losing track of its megastrategy, alienating some of its best customers and responding with contempt to the loyalty of its employees. Now IBM's customers are unhappy, and so are its employees. Can IBM get them back?

## REBUILDING RELATIONSHIPS WITH CUSTOMERS

The most important area for IBM to start rebuilding is in its ties to its customers. Lou Gerstner is customer-oriented. His plan is to return IBM to its megastrategy, renewing the value of singleness in the eyes of its customers. Customers may very well want a greater integration of all the hardware and software thrown at them these days. "We're going to be the company that has the capacity to deliver total solutions," Gerstner has told an interviewer. "I think that, day in and day out, our diversity and our capacity to integrate will be a very powerful tool for us, and for shareholders and customers."[3]

Customers are hungry for a single-solution vendor who can deliver a distributed computing system. Many are unhappy with the integration headaches that a fragmented information-technology industry has been offering them: Information services people cannot make spreadsheets from one vendor work with text-processing packages from another; networking software does not mesh with the workstations and servers; and so on. A single vendor with an integrated product line using the microcomputer as its driver will do very well indeed.

IBM would thus go back to presenting one face to customers. This face may well wear an industry orientation as opposed to a product orientation, and there may be a new marketing structure, but overall there will be one IBM rather than numerous, uncoordinated competing units. "The strategic requirements of this business demand an organization that is not divided into groups of isolated or autonomous units," Gerstner told a reporter. "The profit margins and the speed to market require that we do things once and we do them fast."[4]

An IBM customer responding to our customer-satisfaction survey described the problem. "In the past, IBM set the standards and provided complete solutions for everything. Today thirty to fifty vendors are in the marketplace—all offering partial solutions." Another customer echoed this observation. "What IBM used to give the industry was a consistency in standards and approach. Now, there are ad hoc standards. IBM also offered a cohesive product line. Now we don't have that anymore."

Interestingly, IBM is even returning on a limited scale to a form of rentals. The company now offers customers the opportunity to buy

MIPS (millions of instructions per second) off mainframes owned, maintained, and serviced by IBM. Customers thus have a big incentive to buy IBM peripherals—they're certain to be compatible. It's the old strategy in a new guise, though certainly limited in impact and possibly in potential.

### Focusing on the Largest Customers

IBM's most important customers—the largest companies in most industries—are now moving toward the new paradigm of computing. They're turning toward microcomputer-based networks with larger machines serving as data-storage hubs. In effect, two generations of technology are converging in a post-mainframe configuration: desktop personal computers that maximize individual productivity are joined with mainframes that let thousands of microcomputers store and access large or complex data files and communicate quickly with one another.

IBM has been focusing on the largest firms to rebuild its customer base. This may appear logical, but it risks slapping a new set of blinders on the firm's thinking. In our interviews with smaller firms among IBM's customers, a complaint frequently surfaced. "We invited IBM to be involved with us," said the chief information officer of a medium-sized firm, "but they didn't want to bother with us and many other customers. We got no attention, so consequently we went elsewhere."

IBM's decision to focus on the largest potential customers may have to do with more than size alone. Our customer interviews revealed that the largest customers are making different use of information technology than are medium-sized firms. In essence, the largest firms are using information technology to tie themselves more closely to their customers. Smaller firms are still looking to the new technology to improve internal processes and productivity (for example, in business process reengineering). IBM seems more responsive to the former use than the latter. IBM communicates with its largest customers about their needs and seems to be responsive to them. These customers don't need to ask, "Can IBM understand my firm's needs?" but rather "Can IBM deliver solutions to my firm efficiently?" That is, how well does IBM deliver what it promises? The second tier of IBM's customers, a bit behind the larger firms in their computer use, do ask "Can IBM understand my firm's needs?" That is, does IBM promise the right things?

IBM must be able to consider the needs of all of its customers if it hopes to regain leadership in information technology. It should not try to rely on a few selected relationships as it did in the past. In the future, it is likely that a very large volume of systems sales will be to medium and small firms.

## What Customers Think of IBM

IBM's success in the future depends on regaining the close relationship with its customers that the firm so sadly squandered in the late 1980s and early 1990s. In large part this requires IBM to properly assess its customers' attitude toward IBM. Recognizing the importance of this issue question, we addressed it in interviews with spokespersons for large and medium-sized firms doing business with IBM. Many of the opinions elicited were favorable to IBM; some were not.

Most favorable to IBM, and perhaps most surprising of the responses we received, was the majority opinion that IBM—more than any other information-technology firm—would shape the future success of customers' information systems. We asked respondents to name the two information-technology vendors that they expected to have the most influence on their firms in the future. IBM was cited by 50 percent of the firms; Microsoft was next, cited by 34 percent; Hewlett-Packard was third, cited by 9 percent. Whether it is simply an historical holdover or a valid perception of the current situation, customers and potential customers still look to IBM to determine the future of information technology.

What an opportunity for IBM! It need only seize the new computing paradigm, and it will find a marketplace ready and waiting—and looking to IBM for leadership.

But there are problems. Customers report that IBM promises integration of their customers' various computer systems through incorporation of other vendors' products, if necessary, but that IBM salespeople are woefully ignorant of the offerings of other vendors. IBMers reportedly promise the systems of any vendors, but are willing and able to deliver only IBM. In place of the product and system knowledge crucial in today's marketplace, IBMers often seem to have only time-worn sales techniques. One customer reports having been invited by her IBM sales representative to attend a tennis match. The customer had no interest; she was too busy. The IBMer begged. The customer refused. Finally the IBMer showed the customer a company sheet containing a box that the sales representative had to check off—it referred to entertaining the customer. "If I don't do it," the IBMer explained, "I'll be in trouble at the company." The customer, out of pity, let herself be escorted to a tennis match. Even more serious is the complaint of another customer who told us "IBM's sales force has no idea of the company's vision or strategy. Nor are they being trained in this. The company has been cutting costs ruthlessly, and training has been much affected. But if they don't resume training soon, they won't be able to pump up sales."

Our survey also asked questions about IBM's chances of resuming its leadership position. Most of the larger firms that have historically been IBM's best customers are hopeful. This is striking when one considers the pessimism of the media about the same question and the strong body of opinion in the information-technology industry that sees IBM as a dinosaur. In private conversation, non-IBM executives and investors will often say that IBM is finished; some put it more carefully, saying that Lou Gerstner has a very difficult task ahead of him in trying to revive IBM. In contrast to this pessimism, fully 40 percent of information-technology executives in customer organizations said that they felt IBM's chance of revival to its previous status in the industry was good to excellent; 50 percent said it was fair. Only 10 percent of our respondents classified IBM's prospects as dim.

Why do so many customers have such high expectations? Most take a long view. "It's no different from when AT&T was deregulated," said one executive. "It took a while for the company to learn how to compete. But it did learn. IBM will come back." Said another, "They'll come back. They'll adapt and continue to be a major player." Many customers pointed to the undoubted strengths of IBM. "They have great people and a great name," said one respondent. "IBM has very talented people and is very strong in terms of research and development. . . . It's not too far out of the loop to get back in the game." "IBM has a leg up on many companies because of its vast resources," said yet another. And another added, "IBM has lots of resources, more than all the other computer makers combined. I don't anticipate their demise." Some respondents were very specific about IBM's current products. "I'm excited with their open-systems environment," said one, continuing, "Their personal computer prospects are enormous." Said another, "They have the strongest portfolio of products that I've ever seen."

The customers who thought IBM had only a fair chance of revival based their opinion on the fear that IBM would continue its outdated practices. "They've got the best system," said one, "but they've got to get rid of the people in the company who want exclusive control. They've got to learn how to do it faster and cheaper versus trying to hook people entirely into their system and their system alone." In other words, IBM must succeed in an open-systems environment based on speed and low cost—and not try to reestablish the proprietary systems of the past.

The open-systems environment presents its own challenges, however. "One concern I have," said a respondent from a very large firm, "is that vendors are promising a lot of things that they can't deliver. What's happening is that if the competition says it can deliver something, [IBMers] decide that they should deliver it as well. As a customer, I don't know if I can trust anybody anymore. There's a much greater burden on us to evaluate everything that everyone is offering." In addition, large customers are reluctant to put up with integration headaches. "Who do I call when my system fails—the hardware vendor, the software vendor, the integrator? Why have I got five salesmen sitting in my office? I want information technology that I plug in, turn on, and use!"

It was precisely these burdens of evaluation, integration, and maintenance that IBM, with its traditional singleness strategy, had removed from its customers' shoulders. As the information-technology marketplace gets more complex, IBM's chances of a successful return to its megastrategy increase. What company is placed to offer a single-source solution? Only IBM.

But singleness alone will not be enough. The marketplace is more cost-conscious than ever before. IBM's challenge will be to reduce costs. The same customer who wanted plug-in technology also said "Before, when we bought things from IBM, we knew they would work. Now the burden is on us to put together different parts. It increases the risk, but if it works, it's considerably cheaper."

Perhaps the best summary of the views of IBM's customers was provided by an executive who said,

IBM has the experience and the expertise that many companies can't touch. Other hardware vendors can put out similar stuff, but they don't have the software IBM has. IBM's got the whole spectrum together and can truly market the whole package to me versus working with a hardware vendor and a software vendor. Other companies just have one niche. IBM does it all.

Here was the age-old plea of the harassed executive seeking a one-stop shop. This was the market IBM created and served so successfully for decades. This is the market IBM let lapse in the 1980s and early 1990s. In the mid-1990s that market awaits IBM's return.

## UPDATING THE LOYALTY CONTRACT

If IBM's first priority is to restore its relationship with its customers, then the second priority must be to rebuild its loyalty contract with its employees. IBM's genius has always been in connecting the welfare of the business and to the welfare of the staff. Its megastrategy is a two-legged creature—singleness and loyalty. IBM would be clumsy and inept on only one leg.

The old social contract at IBM tied employees to the firm and made singleness effective. Without the loyalty contract, IBM can still achieve much with singleness: A canoe can be steered, albeit awkwardly, from one side. But the collapse of IBM's old social contract has left the firm demoralized, making the cost-cutting and productivity improvements it needs difficult to obtain.

The social contract affects the customer—and singleness—directly. "What affected me most," one IBM customer at a large firm told us, "was their layoffs. No one at IBM can answer questions anymore. They cut their sales force to cut costs, but there's no one there who knows what's going on. . . . Service from IBM is a lot worse than it was before." IBM's top executives had not expected this response from customers to the layoffs. They had expected that remaining IBMers' concerns for their jobs would lead them to renew their commitment to the firm and to treat customers better, not worse. But almost none of the more than one hundred respondents to our customer survey said that service or sales contacts from IBM had improved.

One measure of the task before IBM in reestablishing rapport with its employees is the radical shift in attitude about the company among former employees. In the past, former IBM employees constituted a potent support group for the firm. Ex-IBMers employed at other firms were usually IBM boosters and, often, customers. They were sometimes referred to as a fifth column by IBM's competitors, who found it difficult to sell to companies seeded with former IBMers. IBM retirees were a potent lobbying force on behalf of the company in the communities in which they lived. IBM executives met frequently with retiree groups all over the world. No company had a closer relationship with former employees than did IBM.

How the situation has changed! Former IBM employees now make up the majority of the National Organization of Downsized Employees, which, among other activities, is pressing claims against the government for refunds of taxes paid by employers on severance pay. The ex-IBMers argue that since IBM required them, in return for severance, to sign waivers promising not to sue the company, the payments were not taxable income but non-taxable damages.[5] Far from a cheering section, IBMers forced out by the company over the past few years constitute an active group of disgruntled people who consider that IBM owed and paid them damages for its failure to honor its full employment practice. These former IBMers are unlikely to tout the company's virtues to their new employers or communities.

Lou Gerstner seems to understand the problem. "What I've found in IBM," he has commented, "is that the very core strengths . . . were still there. . . . We didn't have to change IBM's fundamentals." As if to emphasize this point, so different from the usual view that IBM's technology led to its financial difficulties, Gerstner added, "I've been fortunate enough to have to only work on the behavioral side."[6]

Gerstner has successfully reduced IBM's costs. In 1990, sales, general, and administrative expenses consumed 30 percent of the company's receipt; by 1994, this had fallen to 23 percent. This reduction, and the absence of special restructuring charges, permitted the company to return to profitability in 1994. But cost-cutting has its limits. IBM's leadership must still address the issue so crucial to the firm's future: What will replace the old social contract at IBM?

Most IBMers today have little or no employment security, the traditional benefit of working at IBM, and, because IBM is too large to offer the potential equity gains of a successful start-up, little or none of the possible gain in wealth that small high-tech companies offer. IBM can never be a Microsoft with its numerous millionaire employee shareholders. So why would a talented person go to work for IBM?

This question is not easily answered. Returning to a full employment practice might attract top talent to the company, as it has in the past. People who are much concerned about job security—and IBM has by its past practices assembled a disproportionate number of such people—should not be left without some assurances about their future careers and employment. Leaving them in uncertainty invites demoralization and poor performance. Restoring employment security to IBM's regular employees, but using substantial numbers of temporaries, contract, and contractor personnel for flexibility, might be feasible. One key element of such a policy process would have to be an effective performance appraisal system, the lack of which in the 1980s helped condemn IBM to downsizings. The performance appraisal system must allow managers to rank employees and to identify and fire people who don't work out. A second key element would be adherence to IBM's past practice, in which employees whose jobs were eliminated for whatever reason were reassigned to new positions only if they had performed satisfactorily in their previous positions.

And yet, if IBM did return to a version of full employment, would the other side of the mutual obligation be met? Would employee loyalty be reestablished, given today's economic environment? Having once seen the company abandon full employment, many employees may remain suspicious about the future and all too willing to desert the firm if better opportunities beckon. Even in the days before full employment had been violated, some IBMers did this, greatly damaging the company in the marketplace. In addition, IBM today has billions of dollars in cash, leading wary, demoralized employees to look, perhaps, for more concrete and immediate rewards than security. They may be thinking "We've been badly treated. When does IBM start being nice again?" Would a return to full employment be requited with loyalty employee? Perhaps not.

If not, then IBM faces a real quandary. It can't attract and retain top talent by offering employment security nor by offering upside equity potential. It may be that the labor market—not the product market—presents IBM with its most daunting challenge for the future.

## A LONG-TERM PLAYER IN A SHORT-TERM INDUSTRY

For seven decades IBM has been trying to be a long-term player in an industry focused on the short term. This has led to several of IBM's major problems and has caused investors and the media to misunderstand the firm. In IBM's case, being a long-term player in the information-technology industry has meant repeatedly surmounting the technology cycle to attain market dominance.

Long-term growth is not merely a function of repeated short-run successes. Organizational mechanisms must be in place for handling a steady influx of new people, ensuring that they become a productive force once hired. Leadership must be capable of clearly articulating the firm's mission; and a strong culture of shared beliefs about purpose must be paired with policies and practices that create unambiguous incentives to execute tasks without continuous direction. IBM has had these qualities in varying degrees over its long history.

IBM's long-term perspective required it to maintain funding for research in basic sciences, to foster lasting relationships with its customers, and to plan employees' careers through full employment and promote-from-within policies. None of these practices came cheap, requiring the company at times to forgo short-term profits, and, as we have seen, all have been subject to review and revision in recent years. Basic research is a luxury that few companies can afford, nor does it guarantee successful commercial products. Maintaining strong customer relationships required IBM repeatedly to engineer its customers' migration paths from one generation of computer technology to the next. Maintaining full employment meant that IBM had fewer options for reducing losses during business downturns. The promote-from-within doctrine required the company to make substantial investment in employee development.

IBM's long-term perspective has also been evident in its product plans. Over the years, the company has come up with many grandiose ideas (for example, System Network Architecture) that required customers to wait years before completed products could be made available. While more nimble competitors delivered specific products that met customers' immediate needs, IBM was often late to market because its engineers and programmers were encumbered by managing transitions from one generation of technology to another.

Many firms in today's information industry affirm long-term objectives, but they will with time prove to have been only one-product companies. IBM remains one of the very few corporations that has lived through several cycles of technology—and that may yet surmount another.

IBM today doesn't differ much from the IBM of four years ago. It has laid off many employees and cut its costs, but it hasn't changed its product line or its basic strategy of singleness. The economy has improved, and customers are again buying large computers. IBM's capacity is therefore being better used, and with its costs down, its profit margins are better. In part, Lou Gerstner is now benefiting from the change in direction that John Akers set in motion.

The degree of IBM's future success will depend upon how well Gerstner can meet the key challenges facing the firm. First, IBM must rebuild customer relationships. Second, it must restore, revive, or create an effective new social contract with the firm's employees. And third, it must end years of stagnation by stimulating growth with a new vision for the future.

A substantial run-up in IBM's share price since Gerstner took over as chief executive indicates that investors are beginning to conclude that the latest downdraft in IBM's business cycle is now ending. An investment columnist has even asked, "Has International Business Machines Corporation once again become the stock market's bellwether issue?"[7]

# Lessons for the Large Corporation

W HAT IS the future of large corporations like IBM? To some, they seem relics of an age of less rapid change, less intense competition, and a national rather than global economy. Many old and well-established companies have fallen on hard times in recent decades, and reports of financial losses and staff downsizings at large firms are frequent. Evidence mounts that attaining the scale sufficient to dominate a market leads to a loss of flexibility sufficient to maintain competitiveness. Such conditions make it seem that the large corporation is doomed. Ungainly dinosaurs, they are simply unsuited to markets in which ideas appear one year, are brought to market the next, and become obsolete soon after. Small firms linked together in free-form alliances that tackle complex business opportunities may make more sense than a single large company attempting to mobilize resources on a grand scale.

Does IBM's experience confirm this conclusion? What does it tell us about the prospects of large companies today and in the years ahead? We began this book with several questions about IBM and its recent history, answers to which we have subsequently explored in depth. It may be useful to review and explicitly answer them here, in the context of a general consideration of the future of large firms.

Was IBM a victim of its own success? Unquestionably, yes. Intoxicated with good fortune, the company overreached in the 1980s and paid a bitter price in the 1990s.

Did IBM outgrow the capacity of even the most capable of managers to run it effectively? No. IBM's top executives attempted to manage the corporation from the top, despite its great size and complexity, and in so doing exceeded their capabilities. But IBM—a closely integrated company operating in only one industry, and with effective synergy among its various businesses—requires a high degree of central coordination and direction. Its leadership must attain a judicious blend of decentralized operating management and centralized strategic direction, and in the 1980s, IBM's executives failed to get the mixture right. Different leaders might have done better.

Did IBM's basic management techniques become obsolete in today's work environment? Yes. IBM's lengthy study of problems before decisions could be made; its emphasis on consensus; its interminable executive meetings focusing on ideas and plans rather than operating results; its full employment practice, which became a shield for poor performers—all were rendered obsolete in today's more competitive and rapidly changing business environment. But IBM's basic business strategy, composed of singleness and loyalty—if properly administered—remains as valid today as ever.

Is IBM the victim of a corporate culture that pushed the wrong type of executive to the top? Yes. IBM's chief executives were too inbred; too steeped in the arrogance of success; too certain of their own judgment in periods of challenge. IBM's culture contributed greatly to each of these shortcomings.

Most of IBM's failings were avoidable. IBM's recent financial reversals and layoffs were avoidable. Because IBM's difficulties were largely the result of executives' errors, other large firms may hope that with the right choice of leadership they can remain successful even as they grow.

First and foremost, IBM's difficulties reflected a failure at managing fundamentals. Any business runs on two relationships: with its customers and with its employees. All else, no matter how significant it seems—including shareholder relations—actually just gets in the way. Executives ought to make every decision with the goal of satisfying their customers and employees.

IBM broke its contracts with both its customers and its employees; the whole story of its decline can be told in these terms.

## LEARNING FROM IBM's EXPERIENCE

A number of lessons can be taken from IBM's experience.

### 1. Remember That the Customer Comes First.

Only IBM's customers can decide to let it become larger and more successful. IBM could not itself simply decide to become a bigger company, as it tried to do in 1981. Its customers decided that IBM wasn't worth their patronage, and they ceased to let IBM grow. Somehow, IBM's top executives missed this truth.

In the mid-1980s, IBM's long-standing manufacturing customers in the United States were reeling under Japanese and European competition, yet IBM salespersons were barraging them with demands that they buy expensive new machines. Customers concluded that IBM was gouging them, and they sought alternatives to IBM. This search was made easier by IBM's sales force, who knew virtually nothing about competitors' products, thus driving customers to competitors for information. IBM missed opportunities to effectively criticize competitors' products, and, in addition, when customers bought a competitor's products, IBM representatives did not know how to sell IBM compatibles.

Some customers even told John Akers that he was taking IBM, a national asset, down the tubes. But he wouldn't hear it—neither from them nor from those on his own staff who told him the same thing.

Every change has to come from the customer—it can't come from inside a large corporation. IBM seemed to be saying to its customers, "We need you to buy large quantities of our product to keep our factories operating," and its customers responded, "No."

When IBM switched from renting to selling its equipment, it was seeking to improve its margins at the cost of abandoning long-standing relationships with its customers. Japanese executives often assert that it's more valuable to hold the customer than to maintain profit margins. Once lost, a customer relationship may never be regained. IBM turned this insight upside down—to its ultimate detriment.

Evidence of the inadvisability of taking customers for granted abounds in recent business history. American auto companies failed to provide the small cars that many Americans wanted, opening the door to Japanese competition. In the luxury market, German car manufacturers presumed that their American customers were insensitive to price, again opening the door to Japanese competition. Many business travelers have become convinced that airlines neglect their comfort and gouge them on fares. As teleconferencing improves, business travel may level off or even decline.

Despite these many examples, business executives often fail to imagine themselves in their customers' places, and this shortcoming is magnified in the atmosphere of the large firm. Continual committee meetings, political infighting, and other inner-directed activities consume executives' time, creating a largely self-imposed barrier to contact with any but the largest customers. Overt efforts must be made to meet with customers and to attempt to see the company as its customers do. Decentralization also increases the likelihood of customer contact, since executives in smaller firms are more likely to be in close contact with their customers.

But the large firm need not be at a disadvantage. If it can overcome its self-inflicted blindness, it has many opportunities for eliciting customer opinions that are too expensive for smaller firms to undertake, including consultants, focus groups, conferences, and surveys.

## 2. Never Forget the Customer, Even in Decisions That Aren't Directly About Sales or Marketing.

When IBM embarked on its rapid expansion in the early 1980s, it made what seemed at the time an appropriate financing decision. Needing cash, it sought to increase income from two sources, direct purchase by customers of new IBM products and conversion of rental agreements to purchases. IBM wanted to sell, not rent. Customers were encouraged to buy outright or to lease equipment from IBM's financing unit or from leasing firms (for example, COMDISCO). Either way, IBM got the cash up front.

To IBM, this was simply a financing decision aimed at bringing in the large volumes of cash necessary to fund additional capacity. Some in the company criticized the shift from rentals to purchases, saying that IBM was selling off its future (that is, the steady stream of rental income), but IBM's leadership thought the company could maintain the stream of income through outright sales. What almost no one saw at the time was that the switch from rentals to purchases damaged IBM's relationship with its customers. The change was subtle, but of crucial importance.

When IBM rented to its customers, it maintained its own equipment. Its service people were frequently on the customer's property. Customers had ninety-day cancellation options in their rental agreements, which motivated IBM's salespeople to visit often. IBM thus had its eyes and ears inside a customer's business. It was the rental system that kept IBM close to its customers.

Today, with hindsight, some former IBM executives argue that the company could not have continued to rely on rentals, regardless of its expansion strategy and financing decisions. They point out that since technology was beginning to change rapidly, renting equipment posed growing risks for the company. Under their rental agreements, IBM was responsible for keeping customers technologically up to date, and with technology changing rapidly, the cost of doing so may well have become prohibitive. Rentals were, in fact, risk leases—they placed the risk of changing technology with IBM, not its customers. To escape this risk, IBM established its own finance corporation and financed its customers' purchases of IBM equipment via leases, thus shifting the risk of ending up with outdated technology from IBM to its customers.

The risk argument has merit. Lloyds of London, the insurer, took great losses in the late 1980s on insurance contracts it had written to cover computer equipment that became obsolete. But the argument cannot excuse IBM's performance in the marketplace. The company's stagnating sales and loss of profit margin resulted not from the shift from rental to sales but from the shift in IBM's customer relations. IBM's executives failed to perceive that the sources of the firm's intelligence about customers' preferences were drying up. Had they recognized the situation, they might have successfully dealt with it in any of a number of ways. Many people think of IBM as having out-of-date technology in the early 1990s—but IBM had excellent technology. Its work force was extraordinarily talented, but so deaf and blind was the company to its customers' needs that it was unable to take advantage of its quality skills and products.

Decisions made for reasons having nothing to do with customers often to have a tremendous—and usually negative—effect on them. Corners cut in product design and manufacturing to reduce costs ultimately reduce quality and customer satisfaction. When employees are laid off to cut costs, service suffers. Big firms are particularly susceptible to ignoring customers in such situations because decision-making by various units can be fragmented and remote from the marketplace.

When large firms keep the customer foremost, however, they are often able to cut costs significantly. Chrysler, for example, revised its new product development process in the early 1990s by bringing together representatives of the different business functions (including design, engineering, manufacturing, service, and sales) into multifunctional teams. Forced to work together, they found that their common objectives could best be attained if they gave priority to customer concerns. The result was a new vehicle developed in half the time and at half the cost of a traditional design process.

### 3. Understand Your Business.

IBM's executives thought that the company's relationship with its customers was about IBM's products—but they were wrong. The relationship was about reliable systems and service. Customers bought a partnership from IBM, not simply products. When IBM switched to selling products, its customers quickly realized that other companies sometimes offered cheaper and better ones. They left IBM.

IBM's fundamental misconception about what its customers really wanted from it sank the company. IBM's executives misunderstood the essence of their own business, a recipe for disaster.

Peter Drucker refers to what attracts the customer as the theory of a business. Theodore Leavitt calls *marketing myopia* the belief that a business is about a certain product when it is really about the service that the product provides the customer. All executives are prone to this failing, large firms particularly so. Executives managing from the financials press here and there to cut costs or boost revenues. But why are the sales there in the first place? Years of business with customers doesn't mean that a competitor will not steal them away tomorrow.

The theory of a business needs continual updating in today's environment. Nothing prevents large firms from doing this in any or all of its aspects, but the tendency to see trees and not the forest is often difficult to overcome.

## 4. A Chief Executive Shouldn't Be Part of the Management Team.

Consensus management failed at IBM. John Akers, too much a part of the system, lacked the objectivity necessary to shift the company's direction when it became necessary. Certainly, IBM's early consensus about expansion eroded as evidence of failure mounted, but Akers was still tied both to the strategy and to the chosen method of implementation. Top management meetings with divisional executives who could have blown a whistle were wasted in futile controversies about other issues.

A chief executive must push the firm's strategy but maintain distance enough to evaluate results objectively and to change direction if necessary. Top executives cannot simply be part of the management team; they must be both part of the team and outside of it. The core of successful leadership is resolution of this seeming paradox.

Delegating many decisions to divisional or subsidiary executives can help to achieve the proper balance. A chief executive thus reviews the plans of subordinates and may more freely make modifications. Accountability for results remains with the subordinate, and the chief executive can then review them, acting objectively if results are poor to instigate a change of plans or leadership.

The larger the firm, the more important is the objectivity of top executives. When a chief executive is fully committed to an existing strategy, and the strategy begins to fail, there is no one who can alter course. A large firm will take years to turn around from a significant error; a smaller firm may reverse course much more quickly.

Top executives of large firms seem to have a more complete appreciation of the need for objectivity now than in the past. The downsizing of corporate headquarters to the small staffs necessary to monitor and evaluate the performance of operating units, rather than the large staffs needed to manage the firm's business, has, paradoxically, pushed top executives further from the day-to-day business operation and forced greater delegation of responsibility, permitting greater objectivity at the top.

## 5. Reach Carefully

IBM's determination in the early 1980s to force a decade of rapid growth was at the heart of its failure in the early 1990s. It overreached and then had to cut back, at great cost.

There is no easy way to avoid this danger. Critics insist that a firm's executives should quickly perceive that its strategic plan is overly ambitious and pull back; but many would admire a company's persistence in pursuit of its strategy despite short-term market fluctuations. In fact, a company's failure to meet its growth objectives results more often from failure in implementation than from an overly ambitious strategy.

Large companies with great resources are particularly inclined to the misapprehension that they can shape the marketplace to their desires. What is called strategic planning often has this intent. But influences larger than the corporation affect consumers and drive their behavior.

Scenario-based planning is less likely to lead to failure. A company identifies possible changes in the marketplace and prepares appropriate responses, including any necessary changes in strategy. In a positive development, many large companies have abandoned uni-directional planning in favor of the alternative-scenario approach.

## 6. Don't Try to Resolve a Problem of Strategy with a Reorganization.

John Akers's major strategic failure was to try to solve a business-strategy problem—determining what technology and products IBM ought to offer its customers—with a reorganization. In letting IBM's various product lines battle it out in the marketplace, he sought to avoid a decision by decentralizing. The continual temptation in business to reorganize instead of resolving strategic questions must be resisted. A reorganization should implement a strategy, not substitute for one.

## 7. Struggle Unceasingly Against Bureaucracy.

IBM's history gives repeated examples of business success followed by increased bureaucracy and decreased effectiveness. Can this tendency be overcome?

Business magazines frequently report on companies that have seemingly overcome bureaucratic inertia, for example, 3M, Hewlett-Packard, and Motorola. Remarkably—for the moment—these firms do seem to have fully reinvigorated themselves. But it shouldn't be forgotten that each firm had begun to sink into bureaucratic rigidity before achieving renewal. Bureaucratic attitude, it seems, need not spell a firm's eventual ruin, raising the question, what sparks innovation out of bureaucracy?

A strong-willed chief executive fresh in the job, with the backing of the board of directors and a relatively intact base of culture and resources—a platform on which to stand—can reintroduce an innovative and entrepreneurial spirit. A chief executive unwilling to start the cannibalization of existing products and services for fear of consequences to existing revenues, policies, and people does not belong in the job.

## 8. Opportunities Lost Are the Biggest Consequence of a Failure.

Top executives deciding to press for dramatic change in a company's product line must not fail—failure may leave a company fearful of substantial change for years. This is what happened to IBM with the F/S project.

Management finds very strong temptation to reach for the next step in a product line—even when further steps are becoming increasingly expensive. Efforts to find alternative approaches may sometimes be much wiser.

Today we watch, for example, as semiconductor firms pour vast sums into developing the next generation of silicon chips and even greater sums into new facilities to produce them. Ironically, they see the huge costs involved as an advantage—a barrier to the entry of other firms. But in today's super-competitive business world, a rising barrier is an invitation to entrepreneurs to try to find a path around or a tunnel underneath. The silicon chip may be supplanted by a cheaper, more effective technology, just as networked microcomputers are displacing mainframes. Firms that have dominated chip production and pursue that technology blindly will then be revealed as tied to a particular product, not a market.

## 9. Pay Attention to the Employee.

A company that relies on customer relationships is crucially dependent on its employees. Employees build and maintain customer contacts. In its growth effort, IBM too quickly shifted employees from long-term customer contacts, only to watch the customer relationship dissolve.

Further, a company facing rapidly evolving technology is crucially dependent on its professionals and managers. IBM had supported its people with employment security; when it first modified and then abandoned its commitments to them, morale and productivity suffered.

IBM's experiences teach that, having created a social contract over many decades, a firm can modify the provisions in it only if the modifications are carried out in an appropriate manner over an appropriate period of time.

Social contracts are difficult to amend because they have taken shape over time as employers and employees jointly refine their provisions. They are also deeply ingrained: The strength of a social contract is bound up with a firm's success. A successful firm will attract employees who find comfort within its personnel policies and practices. As the social contract gains strength, the firm may become the choice of *only* that type of employee.

Management thus faces a complex task when it tries to change a social contract. Under certain conditions, with proper preparation, even basic explicit and direct provisions may be changed with limited negative impact on workers' motivation. At other times, even inadvertent changes in what appear to be ephemeral implicit and indirect provisions can trigger negative reactions.

Firms should not attempt to rewrite their social contracts without considering long-term consequences. An effective social contract is a delicate creation, a blend of elements that maintains the loyalty and drive of employees over many years only if it is properly nurtured. Executives could easily destroy a company's future if they make abrupt changes in its social contract in pursuit of short-term profits. The next time a crisis hits the company, its remaining talent might have no incentive to stay and would simply pack up and leave.

When a company abrogates its contract with its employees in order to cut costs, it harvests ill-will and ineffectiveness and may find it difficult to attract and retain top talent.

## 10. Big Firms May Be National Assets.

If excess scale is ultimately to blame for IBM's decline, this finding will have profound implications for the information-technology industry. Economists may conclude that vigorous antitrust enforcement should be pursued to ensure that other companies do not meet a similar fate. But such a draconian solution would leave unresolved the problem of ever-more-expensive research and development. How can firms whose capacity to absorb financial risk is limited by antitrust enforcement keep up with the expanding investment in research and development necessitated by rapidly evolving technology?

Information technology has always been synonymous with market risk. In the 1960s, IBM had to invest just over $5 billion in System/360—a sum equal to the *cumulative* after-tax profit reported by IBM from 1914 through 1961. When IBM's funding needs exceeded the estimates that had been made for System/360, the company avoided technical bankruptcy only by going to the capital markets for an emergency equity infusion.[1] In sharp contrast to the billions spent on System/360, microcomputer hardware took shape in the garages of the founders of Hewlett-Packard and Apple; its early software was written in the apartments of the founders of Microsoft and Lotus; the founder of Dell began marketing PCs by mail from his college dorm room. In the microcomputer world, however, small is no longer beautiful. Intel recently sank $1 billion into a new chip plant, and Microsoft has some 2,000 programmers working on its most recent computer operating system. Form and function are pushing the personal computer down the same path that the mainframe took before it; already the microcomputer is no longer a cottage industry, and before long its investment requirements may rival those of the mainframe.

Capital intensity introduces complications in the process of innovation that cannot be ignored. Firms in capital-intensive industries must make huge fixed-cost investments to support products *before* they attain commercial success. In a rational capital market, only firms that can convince their bankers or shareholders that they will see steady demand for these new products will get approval to build; firms lacking market power cannot offer this assurance. Where does market power come from? Bluntly stated—from scale.

Can an information-technology industry composed of relatively small firms rely on cash-short entrepreneurs, a short-sighted capital market, or the unsteady hand of government to fund innovation? Will consortia led by strong-willed entrepreneurs be able to take the breathtaking risks that single large firms once did, or will they restrict themselves to less bold aspirations? If small firms are less bold in technological advance and government less effective in identifying opportunities, a crucial role in industrial leadership remains for the large firm.

Even though firms in capital-intensive industries develop bureaucratic rigidity as they grow in scale, without scale, their ability to support innovation is sharply restricted. This would seem to be a paradox, but firms such as Exxon, Monsanto, Boeing, DuPont, GM, Ford, and IBM all demonstrate that it is resolvable over time.

## HOW THE LARGE FIRM IS CHANGING

The large firms that are emerging as market leaders in their industries differ in appearance from the monoliths of the past. They are reorganizing themselves to meet the challenges of a new economic era.

IBM, like its counterparts in other industries, has been experimenting with empowerment and teamwork in its core activities and with selective spin-offs of non-core activities. Even basic staff functions like training, compensation, data processing, and telecommunications have been outsourced. These initiatives give the firm an entirely new look—a flattened, more responsive central core populated by teams of executives and employees, intertwined in a web of contractual, partnership, and equity agreements with various business associates and customers. Disappearing in this change are the rigid hierarchy and large unitary structure that marked IBM in past cycles of growth and decline; what has not disappeared is the pillar of singleness.

In this book, we have reviewed IBM's efforts to streamline its organization to meet the demands of today's more rapidly changing and competitive business environment. We have considered the struggles of IBM executives to find the proper balance between centralization and decentralization and between managerial direction and lower-level initiatives. We have seen that such transformations involve both a change in corporate culture and a change in organizational structure: Both are necessary—neither can be effective in isolation. Finally, we have seen that despite a need that became glaringly apparent in the late 1980s, IBM has yet to manage the successful transformation of its culture.

The needed change in culture requires that employees be imaginative, adaptable, and non-bureaucratic—and that they be free to exhibit these qualities in the workplace. Several times in its history IBM has had to find its way toward a less bureaucratic culture. It will be doing so again in the late 1990s. IBM's new chief executive has said that IBM will again be a great company—but not the same great company as before. This book has been a tale of IBM's problems. Its transformation will be another story.

# Appendix

IBM'S Annual Performance against National GDPs

| Year | IBM's Adjusted Income ($ million) | GDP at 1985 Price Levels—USA ($ billion) | GDP at 1985 Price Levels— OECD Europe ($ billion) | GDP at 1985 Price Levels— Japan (trillion yen) |
|------|------|------|------|------|
| 1963 | 199.70 | 2,096.60 | 1,482.69 | 84.09 |
| 1964 | 235.09 | 2,213.90 | 1,569.77 | 93.91 |
| 1965 | 257.37 | 2,336.10 | 1,636.45 | 99.38 |
| 1966 | 278.67 | 2,473.40 | 1,698.65 | 109.95 |
| 1967 | 339.68 | 2,536.40 | 1,754.20 | 122.13 |
| 1968 | 443.51 | 2,641.40 | 1,841.87 | 137.87 |
| 1969 | 460.72 | 2,715.80 | 1,952.08 | 155.07 |
| 1970 | 488.49 | 2,714.40 | 2,046.88 | 171.67 |
| 1971 | 509.85 | 2,791.80 | 2,113.70 | 178.99 |
| 1972 | 595.00 | 2,934.40 | 2,202.86 | 193.71 |
| 1973 | 704.28 | 3,086.60 | 2,330.38 | 208.48 |
| 1974 | 778.66 | 3,069.40 | 2,377.61 | 207.20 |
| 1975 | 819.22 | 3,043.50 | 2,359.04 | 213.12 |
| 1976 | 967.75 | 3,193.80 | 2,462.76 | 222.10 |
| 1977 | 1,068.53 | 3,336.40 | 2,530.81 | 232.57 |
| 1978 | 1,180.48 | 3,490.00 | 2,606.62 | 243.89 |
| 1979 | 1,087.79 | 3,579.20 | 2,699.14 | 257.39 |
| 1980 | 1,174.21 | 3,563.80 | 2,737.97 | 266.74 |

*Continued on next page*

*Continued*

| Year | IBM's Adjusted Income ($ million) | GDP at 1985 Price Levels—USA ($ billion) | GDP at 1985 Price Levels— OECD Europe ($ billion) | GDP at 1985 Price Levels— Japan (trillion yen) |
|---|---|---|---|---|
| 1981 | 1,210.60 | 3,632.90 | 2,744.16 | 276.29 |
| 1982 | 1,459.93 | 3,551.80 | 2,766.40 | 285.02 |
| 1983 | 1,793.66 | 3,675.00 | 2,814.01 | 292.72 |
| 1984 | 2,125.28 | 3,900.70 | 2,884.59 | 305.21 |
| 1985 | 2,090.91 | 4,016.65 | 2,959.40 | 320.42 |
| 1986 | 1,522.25 | 4,119.60 | 3,043.64 | 328.84 |
| 1987 | 1,648.28 | 4,243.30 | 3,129.34 | 342.34 |
| 1988 | 1,795.30 | 4,410.60 | 3,250.51 | 363.59 |
| 1989 | 1,145.73 | 4,525.30 | 3,356.22 | 380.74 |
| 1990 | 1,801.86 | 4,555.00 | 3,451.80 | 400.63 |
| 1991 | (838.37) | 4,496.10 | 3,491.79 | 418.35 |

Regression of IBM's Adjusted Income and GDPs of the United States, OECD-Europe, and Japan

### Regression Statistics

| | |
|---|---|
| Multiple R | 0.6927 |
| R Square | 0.4798 |
| Adjusted R Square | 0.4174 |
| Standard Error | 517.3229 |
| Observations | 29 |

| Analysis of Variance | df | Sum of Squares | Mean Square | F | Significance F |
|---|---|---|---|---|---|
| Regression | 3 | 6171700.2254 | 2057233.4085 | 7.6871 | 0.0008 |
| Residual | 25 | 6690573.9311 | 267622.9572 | | |
| Total | 28 | 12862274.16 | | | |

| | Coefficients | Standard Error | t Statistic | P-value | Lower 95% |
|---|---|---|---|---|---|
| Intercept | −6674.4770 | 2391.9103 | −2.7904 | 0.0094 | −11600.7051 |
| x1 | 2.4082 | 1.1858 | 2.0309 | 0.0519 | −0.0340 |
| x2 | 2.9244 | 2.2340 | 1.3090 | 0.2012 | −1.6767 |
| x3 | −32.4024 | 13.4929 | −2.4014 | 0.0232 | −60.1915 |

# Notes

**Chapter 1**

1. Page 3: Thomas J. Watson, Jr., memorandum, IBM, March 1961, p. 6. First quote on page 4: T. A. Wise, "IBM's $5,000,000,000 Gamble," *Fortune,* September 1966, p. 122. Second quote on page 4, Ibid., p. 54. Quote on pages 4–5, Thomas J. Watson, Jr., memorandum, IBM, n.d., p. 4. Quote on page 6, Wise, "IBM's $5,000,000,000 Gamble," p. 64.
2. "Nerd Instinct," *The Economist,* 10 June 1995, p. 15.
3. Otto Eckstein, personal conversation with D. Quinn Mills.
4. Ken Olsen, personal conversation with D. Quinn Mills.
5. Former union president, personal conversation with D. Quinn Mills.
6. Former IBM CFO, personal conversation with D. Quinn Mills.

**Chapter 2**

1. "GE's Edsel," *Forbes,* 1 April 1967, pp. 21–23.
2. It is likely that the data for 1930–1941, when IBM had the leading tabulator architecture, would show a similar pattern. Although we have the relevant income data for those years, we were unable to obtain inflation adjustments for 1930–1938, so could include only 1939–1941 in the figure. These three years show performance as would be expected.
3. Charles J. V. Murphy, "The U.S. as a Bombing Target," *Fortune,* November 1953, pp. 118, 225.

4. Thomas J. Watson, Jr., and Peter Petre, *Father, Son & Company* (New York: Bantam Books, 1990), pp. 241–242.

5. Charles E. Silberman, "The Coming Shakeout in Electronics," *Fortune,* August 1960, pp. 126–130.

6. T. A. Wise, "I.B.M.'s $5,000,000,000 Gamble," *Fortune,* September 1966, pp. 118–123.

7. Ibid., p. 118.

8. A minor problem, in the form of the Altair home-hobby personal computer, was then just looming on the horizon.

9. Fred Lamond, "IBM Versus IBM," *Datamation,* February 1979, p. 25.

10. "IBM, What Ails You," *Forbes,* 20 August 1979, pp. 138–139.

11. Bro Uttal, "I.B.M.'s Battle to Look Superhuman Again," *Fortune,* 19 May 1980, p. 65.

12. "An Overhaul That Will Strengthen IBM's Hand," *Business Week,* 19 October 1981, p. 42.

13. Jerry Pournelle, "Chaos Manor Gets Its Long-Waited IBM PC," *Byte,* February 1984, p. 24.

14. Mark Dahmke, "The Compaq Computer," *Byte,* January 1983, p. 17.

15. "Inside the IBM PCs," *Byte,* 1986 Extra Edition, Fall 1986, p. 2.

## Chapter 3

1. Thomas J. Watson, Jr., and Peter Petre, *Father, Son & Company* (New York: Bantam Books, 1990), pp. 195–197.

2. Thomas J. Watson, Jr., Management Briefing, no. 6-63, 2 October 1963, p. 3.

3. T. Vincent Learson, *Think,* 1 November 1972, p. 4.

4. John Opel, Management Briefing, no. 1-81, 11 September 1981, p. 1.

5. Joseph Schumpeter (a leading economist of the early twentieth century) refers to this inevitable decay of large firms as the "creative destruction" of capitalism. It is his thesis that as large firms become rigid, they no longer keep pace with their markets and are displaced by more innovative firms, triggering an entrepreneurial renewal that recharges the economy.

6. Watson and Petre, *Father, Son & Company,* pp. 241–242.

7. "Is Perfection Forever?" *The Economist,* 12 February 1966, p. 646.

8. Harold Seneker, "The Empire Strikes Back," *Forbes,* 23 June 1980, p. 43.

9. T. A. Wise, "I.B.M.'s $5,000,000,000 Gamble," *Fortune,* September 1966, p. 120.
10. Bro Uttal, "I.B.M.'s Battle to Look Superhuman Again," *Fortune,* 19 May 1980, p. 66.
11. Robert Sheehan, "Tom Jr.'s IBM," *Fortune,* September 1956, p. 34.

## Chapter 4

1. While today's IT is purchased and not leased, we believe that the underlying philosophy of customer service remains the same. No one will buy a multi-million-dollar computer system without ensuring that the appropriate service and support are available to keep it running.

## Chapter 5

1. See R. Roosevelt Thomas, Jr., "Note on Managing the Psychological Contract," teaching note 474-159, Harvard Business School, 1974, p. 2.
2. Thomas J. Watson, Jr., Management Briefing, no. 9-65, 9 December 1965, p. 4.
3. Thomas J. Watson, Jr., Policy Letter No. 4, 21 September 1953, p. 4.
4. "Careers in IBM," IBM, n.d., p. 3.
5. "Everything You Wanted to Know About Pay," IBM, n.d., p. 23.
6. Scientific management, often attributed to American efficiency engineer Frederick W. Taylor, was further refined under the pressure of the development of automation techniques by Henry Ford and others.

## Chapter 6

1. See IBM's *1993 Annual Report,* pp. 32 and 63, for details.
2. IBM, *1993 Annual Report,* pp. 32, 45–46, and 63. Footnote L offers more food for thought: of the $24 billion in charges, more than $10 billion *remained* to be used at the end of fiscal 1993. In other words, IBM has charged itself $10 billion more than it has spent on restructuring to date.
3. A firm's *operating margin* is the net profit left after all costs of making a product or providing a service are deducted from the revenue received for selling that product or service to a customer. Once the company pays for general and administrative expenses

and other charges out of the operating margin, it can declare the remainder as pre-tax profit.

4. E. Pugh, L. R. Johnson, J. H. Palmer, and C. H. Bashe, *IBM's 360 and Early 370 Systems* (Cambridge, Mass.: MIT Press, 1991).

5. Charles H. Ferguson and Charles R. Morris, *Computer Wars* (New York: Times Books, 1993), p. 176.

6. According to a *Wall Street Journal* article, IBM's turnover rate in the 1960s averaged between 6 percent and 8 percent, while the average at other U.S. companies was around 10.2 percent. It is not clear whether these rates included both voluntary and involuntary turnovers, but in any case they were much mightier than IBM's 2.8 percent voluntary and involuntary turnover rate in 1985 and higher than the rate we used in our estimate. See "It Can Be Wrenching to Quit, but a Few Do," *Wall Street Journal,* 7 April 1986.

7. Thomas J. Watson, Jr., IBM internal memorandum, n.d., p. 3.

8. Tom Melohn, *The New Partnership* (Essex Junction, Vt.: Oliver Wright Publications, Inc., 1994), p. 228.

9. Ibid., p. 214.

## Chapter 7

1. One need only ask Fred Wang of Wang Computer, Ken Olsen of Digital Equipment Corporation, Edson De Castro of Data General, or Rod Cannion of Compaq about this point.

2. Thomas J. Watson, Jr., and Peter Petre, *Father, Son & Company* (New York: Bantam Books, 1990), p. 408.

## Chapter 8

1. According to a story recounted frequently in the press, Microsoft's chairman offered the rights to MS-DOS to IBM and IBM refused to buy them. We can find no confirmation at IBM's highest levels for this supposed offer, but it is possible, IBM executives agree, that such an offer was made to lower-level representatives of IBM and never, apparently, reached the chief executive's office.

## Chapter 9

1. We acknowledge that there are many proponents of the opposite viewpoint, that capital-market discipline has improved corporate performance in recent years.

2. Present-value analysis works as follows: If an investment is expected to pay off in two years, investors use their cost of capital

to discount this return. Say the cost of capital is 10 percent; since the investment is for two years, the investor multiplies 1.10 × 1.10 (because interest rates are stated in annual terms) to obtain a present-value factor of 1.21. If the payment to be received from the investment is a nominal $1,000, then this payment is actually worth $1,000 divided by 1.21, or $826.44, today; if it can be bought for less it is a good deal.

Now suppose another investment, one offering $1,300 in six years, is also available. Is it a better deal than the $1,000? Since the investor's cost of capital today is the same for either investment, 1.10 is multiplied by itself 5 times (to account for six years) to arrive at a factor of 1.61, and the "present" value of $1,300 six years from today is $808 (1,300 divided by 1.610). Obviously, the $1,000 in two years is worth more than $1,300 in six years just as $826 today is more than $808.

This type of investment analysis can be adapted to take account of inflation by using the current term structure of interest rates. The analyst looks into the marketplace for the cost of capital placed for a two-year term and might discover that it remains 10 percent per annum; but in looking at six-year rates, the analyst discovers that the market is demanding 12 percent per annum. (The extra two percentage points are being demanded by investors expecting a rise in inflation over the term of the investment.) Using 12 percent to generate the discount factor in the six-year investment example above yields a denominator of 1.97, making the $1,300 payment worth only $660 today. An investor might have seen little difference between $826 and $808, particularly if he or she felt short-term rates might fall— after all, the two-year money would need to be reinvested twice during the time that the six-year investment would not. But the difference between $660 and $826 is about 25 percent, and the investor will almost certainly take the short investment now. The long term ceases to count.

3. See Paul Gibson, *Bear Trap: Why Wall Street Doesn't Work* (New York: Atlantic Monthly Press, 1993), for a further exploration of these and other ideas about the failure of the capital markets.
4. For example, IBM's market valuation exceeded $70 billion at the end of 1988. The largest leveraged buyout up until then was the KKR takeover of RJR Nabisco, valued at about $25 billion.
5. This was calculated by dividing the split-adjusted IBM stock price by a deflator. The deflator for a given year was calculated by dividing the CPI level for that year by the CPI level of the base year, 1967.

6. This was done by dividing the split-adjusted IBM stock price by a deflator. The deflator for a given year was calculated by dividing the S&P 500 Index level for that year by the S&P 500 Index level of the base year, 1967.
7. Therese Poletti, "IBM Corp. New CEO Faces Major Challenges," Reuters, 26 March 1993.
8. See D. B. Yoffie and A. E. Pearson, "The Transformation of IBM," case 9-391-073, Harvard Business School, 1991, p. 6.
9. Bill Dunne, "A Company Transformed—How IBM Got from There to Here in Six Years," *Think,* no. 5, 1992, p. 7.
10. IBM, internal document, n.d., pp. 2–3.
11. IBM reported $18.486 billion in losses before income taxes from 1992 through the third quarter of 1993. Pre-tax restructuring charges amounted to $20.59 billion, or 111 percent of its losses.

## Chapter 10

1. Diamant Calbour, "New Directions in Compensation and Benefits at IBM," *Journal of International Compensation & Benefits* (July/ August 1992): 13–18.

## Chapter 11

1. *Datamation,* November 1994, p. 24.
2. Ibid.
3. "We Won't Stop . . . ," *Business Week,* 1 May 1995, pp. 117, 120.
4. Louise Kehoe, "Big Blue Drives Back to the Black," *Financial Times,* 5 June 1995, p. 15.
5. Juliet F. Brudney, "Coalition Benefits Older Workers Blindsided by Corporate Downsizing," *Boston Globe,* 28 March 1995, p. 51.
6. "We Won't Stop," pp. 117, 120.
7. Leo Fasciocco, "Is IBM's Rally Casting a Long Shadow?" *Investor's Business Daily,* 26 April 1995, p. 1.

## Chapter 12

1. For more on the drama of System/360, consult Thomas J. Watson, Jr., and Peter Petre, *Father, Son & Company* (New York: Bantam Books, 1990). To put this investment in historical context, the reader must remember that IBM had roughly a 75 percent share

of the IT market in the early 1960s. Given the erosion of margins and the fragmentation of the industry that has taken place since the mid-1980s, it is unlikely that any single firm could undertake a project like System/360 today; the risks would simply be too great for their more slender capital structures.

# Index

# About the Authors

**D. Quinn Mills** is the Albert J. Weatherhead, Jr. Professor of Business Administration at the Harvard Business School as well as a consultant to major corporations and government agencies. Previous to his tenure at Harvard, he taught at MIT's Sloan School of Management and served as chairman of the Construction Industry Stabilization Committee, Washington, D.C. Mills has written more than ten books, including the leading text in labor relations, and dozens of articles. He is widely quoted in the national media.

**G. Bruce Freisen** is a knowledge manager in the Enterprise Transformation Team at Andersen Consulting. He has also been an associate at McKinsey & Company and an associate fellow at the Harvard Business School. Friesen has co-authored book chapters and articles and has written numerous case studies for use at the Harvard Business School and in private management training programs.